Cornish
PIONEERS

Cornish
PIONEERS

AND THE ODD VILLAIN

BOB RICHARDS

The
History
Press

To my Dad

First published 2008
Reprinted 2009, 2024

The History Press Ltd
97 St GEorge's Place,
Cheltenham, Gloucestershire, GL50 2QB
www.thehistorypress.co.uk

British Library Cataloguing in Publication Data.
A catalogue record for this book is available from the British Library.

ISBN 978 0 7524 4713 1

Typesetting and origination by The History Press Ltd.
Printed by TJ Books Limited, Padstow, Cornwall

MIX
Paper | Supporting
responsible forestry
FSC
www.fsc.org   FSC® C013056

Contents

Introduction

Cornwall has always been considered a quite unique part of the world. Evidence of ancient civilisations abounds around us; stone circles, chambered tombs and standing stones give some small insight into the lives of those who were here, perhaps as much as 10,000 years ago. The area we now know as Cornwall was populated by Celtic folk over many millennia whose hard-working ways crafted a living out of a land which for many in later centuries was seen as almost a barren waste. The Romans, for example, did not come this far west in any great numbers, preferring for the most part to halt the advance of their empire around Exeter. They established a fort at Nanstallon on the River Camel and one Roman villa has been uncovered near Camborne but aside from these, little evidence of Roman invasion is to be found. A few hundred years later the Saxons had a go at subjugating the Cornish but again for the most part Exeter was as far as they ruled with any authority. Other invaders have also left us very much alone.

Although lands here were divided as the spoils of war by William the Conqueror and his armies, the chosen place for the seat of government for Robert de Mortain, the first Earl of Cornwall, was Launceston, in the far east of the county and as close to the rest of England as it was possible to get. Ingulf's Chronicle of 1120 records Cornwall as 'a nation distinct from England'. Reginald, Earl of Cornwall, grants a charter to his 'free burgesses of Triueru', (Truro) in 1173, and he addresses his meetings at Truro to 'All men both Cornish and English' suggesting a continuing differentiation. Reginald's Charter for Launceston continues that distinction with phrases such as 'To all my men, French, English and Cornish'. So to find then that there is a Cornish identity surviving even to this day is no real surprise.

Down the millennia, whilst others were busily engaged in fighting amongst themselves, the Cornish were to be found basically minding their own business and getting on with earning a living which for many meant digging holes in the ground and coming up with all sorts of useful metallic ores like tin and copper, for example, which sparked off the Bronze Age. Word spread about this commodity as far as some of the ancient civilisations of the Mediterranean region and they came here to trade. It is the mining of these and other ores which has, for the most part, given Cornwall its income down many centuries and when these commodities became harder to reach, the Cornish came up with new ways of reaching them. Steam power for example was pioneered in Cornwall, despite what others might claim. Solving the problems of digging out ore from ever increasing depth and difficulty was, however, not enough and the nineteenth century saw a general decline in Cornish mining fortunes. But its folk did not sit around and lament the bygone age, instead they took their skills and their knowledge to other parts of the ever expanding world where new mines were being opened up. Places like North America, South America, Australia and New Zealand were soon hearing the distinctive Cornish dialect as they developed from newly discovered colonies into wealthy nations. The exploits of many Cornish folk during this period are well documented but here in the pages which follow, I have endeavoured to discover new pioneers, some of whom were of the great mining age but some who have made their mark, quietly and almost anonymously, in a variety of ways in a variety of places. Stories of these Cornish pioneers have been gleaned from my work as a family history researcher, delving into the Cornish families of folk from all corners of the modern world. These twenty-first-century folk have been gracious enough to allow me to share in the stories of their families which they themselves have researched since the days when their forebears left Cornwall. To them, for their interest and their stories, I acknowledge a great debt of gratitude. I hope that their stories will interest all, both Cornish and non-Cornish, and give a small flavour of Cornish influence in a variety of ways across the world.

one

Harvey, Hicks and Jose
Three Miners and an Architect

It is strange sometimes how lives which begin some miles apart are interwoven by circumstance, fortune and fate. Such is the case of three Cornishmen, all of whom made their fortunes in South America and invested them at a later date back home in Cornwall.

The first of these was Robert Harvey. He was the second son of Samuel and Emma Harvey and was baptised in Kenwyn Church, Truro on 14 November 1847. Samuel and Emma had nine more children after Robert, their family eventually totalling seven sons and four daughters. Emma was formerly Emma Northey before her marriage to Samuel in 1845 and both the Harvey and Northey families had lengthy associations with the Truro area. The 1861 census shows the family living at Higher Town, Truro and gives Samuel's occupation as 'collector for news papers'. It seems that Samuel may have had several different occupations in his lifetime as other records show him variously as a tailor and as an accountant. However, the 1861 census has his son Robert as a 'scholar, aged 13'.

Soon after this, Robert was engaged as an apprentice in a Truro iron foundry which made machinery and tools for the mining industry. He later transferred to the much bigger Williams Perran Foundry at Perranarworthal, about five miles out of Truro, and it was here that he became a skilled and respected craftsman. Perran Foundry was at this time one of the two largest and most productive foundries in Cornwall, making some of the huge beam engines, boilers and other machinery used in the mines. It began life under the Fox family, a family of Quakers in 1791, according to the semi-elliptical arch still visible above one of the doorways of the now crumbling buildings. The Williams family of Scorrier were great benefactors of mining and they were involved in the foundry at Perran from its earliest days, eventually taking a major ownership share.

As well as supplying the needs of the Cornish mining industry, Perran Foundry had customers across the vast Atlantic Ocean in places as far away as Mexico, Chile and Bolivia, where many Cornishmen had gone to seek new mineral wealth when Cornwall's mines began to suffer their dramatic decline.

As early as 1824 records exist of a shipment of 1,500 tons of mining equipment from Falmouth to Real de Monte in Mexico, including nine steam-driven mine engines. The bulk of this equipment was manufactured at Perran Foundry. Another shipment from Falmouth to Mexico in 1831 of a 36in pumping engine manufactured at Perran Foundry which cost £3,600, equivalent today of about £250,000, ended in disaster when the ship carrying the engine was wrecked off the Mexican coast and the precious cargo was lost.

Early in the 1870s the foundry received an order for an engine from the Tocopilla Copper Mine on the Pacific coast of Chile which was operated by Cornishmen Samuel Lean and John Jose. Robert Harvey was engaged to accompany the engine and his services would be retained by Lean & Jose on contract for three years to ensure the safe and smooth instalment of the new engine, its running and maintenance.

His salary was to be the equivalent of around £700 per month by today's standards rising to nearer £900 if all went well, which it did. This was a huge sum in those days when the average Cornish miner was still counting his weekly wage in mere shillings and pence.

Perran Foundry, where Robert Harvey served his apprenticeship and which produced machinery for mining operations all over Cornwall and exported machinery and technology all over the mining world. Sadly the buildings now lie in a ruined state, despite efforts over recent years to redevelop the site as a heritage museum. (Bob Richards)

When his contract ended, Harvey moved north to the area around Iquique, which was already a centre of nitrate production. This was a far cry from his native Cornwall being adjacent to the Atacama Desert, one of the hottest and driest places on earth. However, it seems that the lure of the nitrate and the salary offered to manage its production were incentives enough to keep him there. He found himself mixed up in the War of the Pacific between 1879 and 1883 when Bolivia and Peru combined forces against Chile in a conflict over the mineral-rich areas around the Peruvian province of Tarapaca and the Bolivian province of Litoral. Chile won both provinces and their mineral wealth, leaving Peru a little smaller and a lot poorer and Bolivia as a landlocked country.

It did not seem to matter to Robert Harvey who ran the country – he simply went from working for one government to offering his services to the victors at a greatly enhanced salary.

By the time he returned to Cornwall to live he was a very wealthy man. He purchased an estate here and various properties around Totnes in Devon and also had a base in London's fashionable St James Square.

He made a failed attempt at becoming MP for Truro but did become president of the Royal Institution of Cornwall and it was he who presented the huge portrait of the Cornish giant, Anthony Paine, which still forms an impressive exhibit at the Royal Cornwall Museum. He held the office of high sherriff of both Cornwall and Devon in successive years in the late 1890s, was a magistrate in both counties and was knighted in 1901.

Our second Cornish entrepreneur came from even more humble beginnings. He was John Jose, born in 1836 the son of a miner from the parish of Gwennap. He was living at Vogue, St Day at the time of the 1841 census with his parents William and Elizabeth, brothers William and Henry and sister Elizabeth. Other children were to follow including another brother, Joseph. He and his brothers followed the family tradition of mining locally but in later life worked in Mexico, Chile and Bolivia. Here he, together with Henry, William and Joseph, joined an ever increasing Cornish enclave working the silver mines in the Chanarcillo district, later purchasing copper-mining interests for themselves on the Chilean coast. As we have noted previously all was not peace and tranquillity in this area at the time and sadly, John's brother Henry was killed in 1858 during an attack by Army mutineers. The fortunes of the remaining brothers were soon made in the hugely profitable Tocopilla district where they initially mined copper and later also built a smelting works for the ore. They brought over steam-powered engines built at Perran Foundry and with these engines came Robert Harvey who we have previously met. Running these was quite a problem initially as there was a scarcity of fresh water and it had to be brought to the mine site on mule trains until a method of taking the salt and other impurities out of the sea water was developed. Being on the coast, this commodity was in plentiful supply. Lean, Jose & Co. became a very wealthy company, Lean being Samuel Lean, a Cornish cousin of the Jose family. Samuel Lean soon returned to his native Cornwall a rich man but John Jose remained in South America for a few more years. The company was eventually sold and John Jose also returned to live in his native Cornwall. He, like Harvey, bought property here. His estate was at Mellingey in Perranarworthal parish, just a few miles from his birth place in Gwennap. He retained his interest in mining matters and became a shareholder in several mining concerns and ancillary enterprises, including an explosives company. He gave generously to the community in which he lived, and his name can be found still on one of the foundation stones of the Perranwell Wesleyan Chapel with a rather faded date of 7 April 1879, and on the former reading rooms which were built in 1887. Both the chapel and the reading rooms are built on land which was formerly owned by Jose which he gave to the village. John Jose died in 1895 and a large memorial to him can be seen in St Piran's Churchyard, Perranarworthal. Tales of summer picnics at Mellingey long after the death of John Jose are told fondly by the older generation of local folk. Sadly the house itself was destroyed by fire in 1940, the burnt-out shell remaining for a few more years until it was demolished as it was unsafe.

The monument in Perranarworthal Churchyard which commemorates John Jose and other members of the Jose family. (Bob Richards)

The third of our self-made fortune seekers was George Hicks. He was the son of Richard and Elizabeth Hicks and was born in Newquay in 1833. The 1841 census tells us that he also had several siblings, Ann, Henry, Ellen, Catherine, Jane, Hannah and Naomi and that his father was a maltster. George received a formal education, unlike John Jose, but, as with Jose and Harvey, his fortune was to be made not in Cornwall but across the Atlantic Ocean. He was in America at the time of the civil war there and decided that Peru was a better option. Here he founded the basis of his wealth in the nitrate industry, as did Robert Harvey. War and conflict seemed to follow him as he was here in South America at the time of the War of the Pacific, and in fact it was partly his nitrate discoveries in the inhospitable Atacama Desert region that sparked the war between Chile, Bolivia and Peru. He helped in the development of a major port at Antofagasta to handle this new-found dual wealth of the area, nitrates and copper. He was the subject of an arrest warrant in 1879 and fled the area, returning to his native Cornwall. His wealth, as with Jose and Harvey, bought him property in Newquay. He had his mansion, Pentowan, designed by the leading Cornish architect, Sylvanus Trevail. It still stands commanding views over Newquay harbour and the sea and is now a care home. George Hicks retained his contacts in South America and when the troubles had died down, he revisited the area and as well as his nitrate interests, he also developed and helped fund a large coal-mining concern, the Arauco coalfields some 500 miles further south on the Chilean coast from his main nitrate interests. An integral part of the development of this coalfield was the construction of a railway line across some extremely challenging terrain in this mountainous part of Chile. His retirement brought him back to Cornwall and this is where he renewed his acquaintance with Sylvanus Trevail and where we link together all of these and other self-made Cornishmen.

Perranarworthal Parish Church, dedicated to St Piran, the patron saint of tinners. (Bob Richards)

Trevail was born in Luxulyan in 1851. He had already made a considerable mark on Cornish architecture. He designed many schools, which were built following the Education Act of 1870 which created board schools and gave free education to all. He formed a close association with the entrepreneur John Passmore Edwards, another self-made man from humble Cornish beginnings who had made his money in the newspaper industry and who had also been a MP and had dedicated his later life to being something of a champion of the working classes, funding libraries, schools, hospitals, convalescent homes, art galleries and other public buildings. Trevail was the architect of many of these.

But it was in the fledgling tourist industry that Messrs Harvey, Jose & Hicks came together with Trevail. A railway link direct to London and the rest of England had come to Cornwall as far back as the late 1850s and early 1860s when Isambard Kingdom Brunel and others had done their bit to put Cornwall on the map. Tourism was not then for all and sundry but was the province of the wealthy few, who liked to take the sea air away from the dirt and grime of Victorian cities. They also liked to be assured of all the home comforts when travelling and so it was that large and very grand hotels were built to accommodate them. Most of these were situated within easy reach of the railway network as this was the most modern and by far the quickest way to make the journey from London and other cities to Cornwall. Hotels such as the Headland and Atlantic in Newquay, Pendennis in Falmouth and the Carbis Bay Hotel near St Ives were all served by the railway. Some were situated a little further from rail links but were, for the Victorian traveller, nevertheless well within their compass. Housel Bay at The Lizard and King Arthur's Castle at Tintagel were still coastal if not directly served by rail links. Delabole was as close as Tintagel ever got to being a railway town and Helston served The Lizard Peninsula. These hotels, designed by Trevail who often became an integral part of the senior management team, were all under the wing of the Cornish Hotels Co. which Messrs Harvey, Jose & Hicks helped to fund. John Jose was chairman of that company for a while right up to his death.

We have then, three self-made men from different backgrounds and different parts of Cornwall, all of whom made their fortunes and knew each other through their connections with South America, all of whom came back home to their native Cornwall in their later years and all of whom then became associated with Cornwall's most famous architect, together greatly advancing the burgeoning tourist industry upon which Cornwall has come to rely in later decades.

two

Isaac Killicoat
Pioneer from Perranwell

On 22 April 1810 a baptism took place in the Parish Church of St Piran in the village of Perranarworthal about five miles from Truro. Isaac, the son of Isaac and Susanna Killicoat, was baptised. He was about four months old at the time, his date of birth being 9 December 1809.

Isaac senior was a miner, originally from St Agnes on the north Cornwall coast, and his wife, Susanna, formerly Susanna Rowe, was originally from Tregony, which was once an important port and crossing point on the upper tidal reaches of the River Fal.

Isaac senior was baptised on 27 May 1776, the sixth of seven children of John and Mary Killicoat (formerly Lockett) who had married in St Agnes on 29 March 1758, the other children being Abraham, 1758, Ann, 1762, Mary, 1765, Charles, 1767, Jonathan, 1771 and Jacob, 1780.

The family name of Killicoat had, with a variety of spelling interpretations, been in and around the St Agnes area for at least 100 years before the time of Isaac and Susanna. The oldest surviving parish registers for St Agnes date from the 1650s and here in the baptisms we find Elizabeth, 1654, John, 1657 and Charles, 1660, all children of Richard Kellicoate as it was spelt at the time.

Detail on some of these older parish registers is very sparse and nothing is known for certain about the occupations of these earliest family members but it is reasonable to assume that they were involved in mining as this was the major employer in the area and was certainly the occupation of later generations like John Killicoat and his son and grandson who followed him.

These were very harsh times in Cornwall. The wages of miners were very poor and the working conditions often very harsh. Little wonder then that miners are often to be found in the Quarter Sessions record books for what seem to us today to be very insignificant offences. Punishment was also harsh and often carried out in public as a warning to others.

The Michaelmas Quarter Sessions held at Bodmin on 6 October 1785 are no exception. The justices included such prominent Cornish citizens as Sir John St Aubyn, Sir Francis Bassett, Francis Rodd, John Rogers, Henry Hawken Tremayne, John Cory and William Sandys, all of them wealthy men who had made most of their fortunes as mine owners and businessmen.

Among the defendants, crimes and punishments we find the following:

* John Rawling of Mawgan in Pydar, accused of stealing one pair of worsted stockings value 2d from William Bant, sentenced to a public whipping at Polgooth.
* Mary Hearl of Morval, spinster, accused of stealing one linen apron valued at 1d from Ann Knight, sentenced to a public whipping and one year's hard labour in the house of correction followed by a further whipping before her discharge.
* George Ham of Kea, accused of stealing one shirt valued at 6d from William Salmon, sentenced to 21 days in the Bridewell with hard labour.
* John Killicoat of St Agnes, accused of stealing one piece of oak timber from Francis Cole. Acquitted.

Above left: Isaac Killicoat.

Above right: Mary Killicoat, Isaac's second wife.

❖   William Cocking on the same charge, found guilty and sentenced to a public whipping at North Downs Mine.

Even the Killicoat family then were not immune from wrongdoing and although John was found not guilty, his appearance must have been a cause of great concern for his family and would also have meant the loss of at least a day's wages and possibly more as he would undoubtedly have walked to Bodmin from St Agnes, a distance of some thirty miles each way to make his court appearance. He may even have been in custody for a period before the hearing, with the loss of even more precious wages and further hardship for his family.

The family move from St Agnes to Perranwell was to prove beneficial to Isaac Killicoat junior. He was a boy who showed much promise. Free education for all was still many years in the future but Isaac was given lessons from his early years and became quite knowledgeable in a variety of general schooling subjects, and perhaps more importantly in the skills of mining. It was probably his father's influence and authority which saw him receive an education. It would seem that Isaac senior wanted to bring out the best in his family and not allow them to, as he and his father before him had done, work endless years deep underground.

Nothing is known for certain of the young boy's educators. It is unlikely that he attended the long-established grammar school at Truro or that he attended the grammar school in Falmouth which was founded in 1824. It is more likely that he attended a small private school. These were often associated with local parish churches, such as Gwennap, which was within a couple of miles of his home at

Right: Philip Lander Killicoat, son of Isaac and Ann, born in Perranwell on 28 August 1844, baptised on Christmas Day 1844 at Perranarworthal Parish Church, Cornwall. He tragically died in Burra, Australia of injuries sustained in a fall from his pony trap in September 1911.

Below: The wedding photograph of Ruth Killicoat, daughter of Philip Killicoat and granddaughter of Isaac Killicoat who married Norman Hiles Pearse in 1907 at St Mary's Church, Burra, Australia. The photograph is taken on the steps of the Killicoat family home at Abberton Park. One of the young men at the sides of the photograph is Philip Darby Killicoat, who served in the First World War in the Australian Light Horse Regiment but was killed in action on 19 September 1915 at the age of just twenty-four. He is buried in the East Mudros Military Cemetery near Lemnos in Greece. (My grateful thanks to the Burta Community Library, South Australia, for supplying these photographs and for their permission to reproduce them here)

Greenwith Common, Perranwell. The school there was run for many years by a churchwarden, Mr Whitburn, before the days when education acts and board schools made education compulsory and available to all. A school for the sons of mine agents and others who wished to secure a good education for their families was set up at Trevarth in Gwennap in 1835 but this would have been after the time when Isaac was being educated.

By his late teenage years, Isaac Killicoat was beginning to make his mark as a mining man. He soon became surface captain of the great Tresavean Copper Mine in Gwennap parish and had over 500 men under him in this post. He held this position for nearly twenty years. On 6 June 1833 he married Ann Rowe in the parish church of St James in Tregony. She was from Tregony, the same home parish and indeed the same family as his own mother.

The 1841 census of Greenwith Common, Perranwell, which is within the parish of Perranarworthal, shows the following family:

Isaac Killicoat, 30, Agent, Copper Mine, Ann Killicoat, 30, Susan Killicoat, 5, John Killicoat, 3, William Killicoat, 6 months and William Lander, 20, Carpenter.

They were living at Rose Cottage, between Greenwith Common and Rissick, an area I know well from my own childhood days in Perranwell. The house is still standing, although much improved and extended since the days of the Killicoat family. The 1841 Tithe Map of the area shows the property as a house and garden and has Isaac Killicoat junior occupying the property on a lease from its owner, the Earl of Falmouth.

One passing note on the family: Susan, shown here as aged five, was in fact the second child born to Isaac and Ann – an older sister of the same name was baptised on 2 March 1834 and died as an infant, quite a common occurrence at this time when medical provision, even for families of some standing and wealth, was quite poor. Near to them at Greenwith Common lived Ann's parents: John Rowe, fifty-five, mason; Elizabeth Rowe, fifty-five; Elizabeth Rowe, fifteen; Mary Lander, thirty-five; Elizabeth Lander, one; and just a few houses from them: Isaac Killicoat, sixty, miner in copper mine; and Susan Killicoat, sixty.

So here in these three entries we have Isaac senior with his wife, Susan or Susanna, his son, Isaac with his wife Ann and young family, the Rowe family into which the Killicoats had married, and also an interesting link to the family name of Lander. Elizabeth Lander was the wife of Philip Lander, a carpenter. Many of the Lander family were carpenters and joiners and were originally from the St Ives area. No direct link has been established with the more famous Lander brothers of Truro who explored Africa in the early years of the nineteenth century.

Soon after this census, Isaac senior died. He was buried in the churchyard at Perranarworthal on 5 November 1842. His headstone, situated at the eastern end of the church, also commemorates his wife, Susanna as well as Elizabeth and John Betsworth Rowe, his sister-in-law and brother-in-law. Three more children were born to Isaac and Ann over the next few years: Philip Lander Killicoat, born on 28 August and baptised on Christmas Day 1844, Maria Louisa born in 1847 and Elizabeth in 1848.

Meanwhile on the other side of the world in South Australia in 1845, a sheep farmer, William Stear, and another man, Thomas Pickett, had made discoveries which would profoundly affect the lives not only of the Killicoat family but of hundreds of thousands of others from Cornwall and other parts of the British Isles. They had discovered vast reserves of copper ore. The former sheep-farming area known as the Burra was transformed almost overnight into a very significant copper-mining area. Towns were springing up to take the influx of miners and other workers – town names such as Redruth and Aberdeen were evidence of where these folk had come from. The whole area was immensely rich in ore but needed more than its natural resources and the hard graft of the pick and shovel miners to make it pay. It needed the skills of engineers, surveyors and managers to ensure that the work was carried out properly and, most importantly, profitably.

So it was then that soon after baby Elizabeth was baptised, Isaac Killicoat was to leave Perranwell. He was offered employment with John Schneider & Co., later to be known as the Patent Copper Co., in South Australia. This was not an opportunity which a man with Isaac's reputation and obvious hunger for a challenge was to turn down.

He sailed aboard the *Abberton*, a ship which made an annual voyage from England to Australia for several years around this time, taking mainly working-class folk looking for a new life in this emerging new country. The voyage to Australia at the time was usually one of around three months, but being a sailing ship, could not be predicted accurately. In 1848 the *Abberton* under Captain William Carr left London bound for Plymouth where she departed on 24 April. She arrived in Port Adelaide some fourteen weeks later on 3 August with about a dozen cabin passengers and a further sixty in steerage class. The 1849 voyage was nearly a week longer from 5 July to 22 October, with two cabin passengers and a further seventy-eight in steerage. In 1850, the journey was again nearly fourteen weeks. The passengers on this particular trip were so impressed by the overall standards of the ship and its crew taking them to a new life that they wrote a letter to Captain John James, who had taken command from Captain Carr in which they offered 'our most unbounded thanks for the kindness we have at all times received during a long and tedious voyage' and they thanked his crew for 'our quick and prosperous voyage'.

News of safe arrival in Australia would have taken months to reach family back home in England as it could only be conveyed by ships on the return journey. Local newspapers of the time ran columns reporting sightings and news of ships which passed each other at various points on some of these long voyages. Often entries like 'Abberton passed Gibraltar on 20 May' were to be found. News was conveyed to a homebound ship from one outbound and then through newspapers on that ship's arrival in Falmouth or another home port.

News of Isaac's safe arrival would have cheered his wife and young family back home at Greenwith Common where the census of 1851 shows: Ann Killicoat, forty-one, mine agent's wife with children, Susan Ann, fourteen; John, twelve; William, ten; Philip Lander, six; Maria Louisa, three; and baby Elizabeth, two. Isaac's mother Susanna was still living close by at Greenwith Common as a lodger in the household of Sally Mills, a washerwoman, but Susanna was now quite elderly and she died in 1852 and was buried at Perranarworthal on 14 May of that year.

Returning though to events in Australia, the mine manager of the Patent Copper Co., Gregory Seale Walters, had engaged the services of a surveyor, Gavin David Young, himself an immigrant who came from England in 1847 aboard the *Theressa*. This was another of the many immigrant ships typical of the time which on this 1847 voyage brought a total of nearly 240 souls to a new life with male occupations listed as: thirty-three agricultural workers, thirty-two miners, five carpenters, three masons and bricklayers, a blacksmith and a shoemaker. Female occupations included thirty domestic servants and four dressmakers. Their journey had taken 104 days and along the way three small children had died and been buried at sea and four babies had been born.

Gavin Young surveyed a new overland route from the mine site at Kooringa to Port Henry and by using this made a considerable saving in time and money for the company in getting its ore to port ready for trans-shipment. Overland transport back in these early days was mainly by bullock cart.

The new settlements around the Burra area were buzzing with activity and development. By 1852 the population of the area had grown from a few scattered farmers just seven years or so before to around 5,000 souls, almost all of whom were in some way dependant on the copper mining for their employment, whether directly or indirectly. The area needed, more now that at any time, a steady hand at the helm to help steer a profitable course.

Isaac Killicoat played no small role in this. He surveyed and encouraged ever more exploration for new sources of ore in the area as well as having a hand in expanding the road network in his capacity

The headstone in Perranarworthal Churchyard which commemorates Isaac Killicoat's parents and his brother- and sister-in-law. (Bob Richards)

as a member of the Road Board and later the Burra Railway Board. He even went to Montevideo in Uruguay in 1853 to supervise the purchase and transportation of 180 mules and their handlers which were imported into Australia by the Patent Copper Co. to help transport ore from the mines to the smelting works. The journey back to Australia via Cape Horn was beset by bad weather and took seven weeks to accomplish, during which time several of the mules died. When working in the ore fields, these mules could carry at least 2cwt of ore each over some very rough terrain which was too rough for horses or even oxen to be used.

Isaac stood for the Legislative Council and was elected as a member of the Burra District Council, later to become its chairman. His overall contribution to the life and economy of the Burra area of South Australia is one which has led to him being described as 'saving the territory from bankruptcy' through his skill as a mining engineer, encouragement of others and through his work on the local councils and legislative bodies.

His family had joined him in South Australia in 1854 sailing aboard the *Malacca*. By this time, Isaac was well settled and had built a home for them, which he called Abberton Park, named after the ship which had brought him to Australia. Sadly his wife, Ann, died quite young. He remarried in 1868 by which time his expertise was well respected in a far wider area than the Burra. He visited other parts of Australia to advise on the development of mining and also paid visits to New Zealand and the Pacific islands of New Caledonia to impart his vast knowledge to mine owners there. In his later years, Isaac Killicoat retired from mining and led a quieter life at Abberton Park where he ran a sheep farm and had a much celebrated orange orchard. A lifelong member of the Church of England, he died on 18 January 1886. He was buried in Burra Cemetery, survived by two sons, three daughters and twenty-two grandchildren.

One of his sons, Philip Lander Killicoat, took over the running of the extensive sheep farm at Abberton Park and he, like his father before him, also had an active interest in community affairs. He was a long-serving member of the local hospital board and was elected mayor of Burra in 1887 and 1888. He was tragically killed in September 1911 in an accident with his horse-drawn trap. His obituary report states that: 'one trace had dragged and the horse had pulled the trap with only one trace. On reaching the shallow creek the horse appears to have trodden on the hanging trace and suddenly stopped, throwing the deceased out. The horse broke free and walked slowly home.' Philip Killicoat was not so lucky, he was discovered unconscious with severe head injuries and taken to his home but despite the best efforts of the local doctor, he died a few hours later.

Another tragedy would also soon strike the Killicoat family.

One of Isaac's grandsons, Sergeant Philip Darby Killicoat, son of Philip Lander Killicoat, served with honour in the First World War in the Australian Light Horse Regiment but was killed in action on 19 September 1915 at the age of just twenty-four years. He is buried far from his home in the East Mudros Military Cemetery near Lemnos in Greece. Isaac's last resting place is also far from his childhood home in Perranwell but I am sure that in his later years, the thoughts of this kindly looking, stockily built and bearded man would have turned to those places he knew from his early years: the fields and streams of Rissick and Perranwell, where he undoubtedly spent many hours as a child, probably fetching water for the family home from the spring still known locally as Jacob's Well; the gently rolling hills visible from Greenwith Common; the walk each Sunday from his home down the hill through the village and up to the church and even the four miles or so he would walk each way most other days of his young working life from Greenwith across to Gwennap and the Tresavean Copper Mine – these memories I am sure would have had a permanent place in his heart.

My grateful thanks to the Burra History Group for supplying some of the details of the Killicoat family.

three

John Goyne
St Agnes Gold Rush Pioneer

Many Cornish miners were among the first to exploit the mineral riches of the state of Victoria in the south of Australia and we have already noted one such man, Isaac Killicoat of Perranwell, and his contribution to the mining industry in that area. His family were originally from St Agnes on the north Cornish coast and another St Agnes man was also destined to have an equal, if not greater impact on this area.

He was John Goyne or Goyen, depending on which records you look at. As with all names of this era, spelling interpretation varies depending on who is making the entry in the baptism register, marriage register, census form or whatever. Most folk had no formal education so the making of a mark instead of a signature is a common sight and if the curate or the census enumerator made a mistake, you had no means of telling him that he was wrong because you could not read what he had put down or write it correctly for yourself. Similarly the remembering of age and birthdays was of far less importance back then than it is to us nowadays and so when it came to the first full census of England and Wales in 1841 the enumerators were instructed to be accurate with age, where known, otherwise be accurate to the nearest five years, hence the predominance of folk with '5' or '0' on their age on that census. This can also give the impression of an epidemic of twins and triplets in some families with two or three children given the same age. Not so, this is just a sign that the parents were not sure and age was rounded to the nearest five years. All this leads to an immediate problem when looking at the parish registers for places like St Agnes for here we find baptisms, for example, of: John Goyne, son of William Goyne and Betsy baptised on 10 April 1824; John Goyne, son of James Goyne and Elizabeth baptised on 18 December 1826.

So which is the right John Goyne for us? Given that baptism usually took place within a few weeks of birth and then looking further ahead to census records and his given age at death of eighty-one years in 1907, it would seem that the right John for us is John, son of James and Elizabeth, baptised 18 December 1826.

The family name of Goyne can be found amongst the earliest surviving parish registers for St Agnes and there were many Goyne families in St Agnes around this time. Taking the name of William Goyne as just one example, we find marriages in St Agnes as follows around this time:

William Goyne married to Betsy Langdon, 31 August 1823
William Goyne married to Mary Stephens, 8 December 1823
William Goyne married to Mary Peters, 27 December 1823
William Goyne married to Catherine Tonkin, 25 February 1833

and another five marriages of men by the name of William Goyne or Goyen before 1841.

All no doubt in some way related and what is also evident from census and other records is that almost without exception the Goyne family were miners. As with a lot of mining families, life was very harsh and often cut short by accident or illness. 'Miner's lung' was a disease which accounted for many and a miner of above fifty years of age was an old man.

The Goyne family were not exempt from this rule and John's father, James Goyne, died at the age of thirty-four and was buried on 13 December 1833 in St Agnes. The 1841 census tells us that John's widowed mother, Elizabeth, was running a boarding house at Polbrean, St Agnes and that John had a younger sister, Mary aged twelve, and two younger brothers, James aged nine and Francis aged six. It is an interesting household at the time of this census with a variety of boarders, some of whom are miners but also John and Margaret McColl, needlemakers, originally from Scotland, and James Washington a sailmaker, born in 'foreign parts' as was his wife, Ann. There is also a shoemaker and a spinner living here, quite a mixture of trades, but all very valuable in an area where mining and the sea played very important roles in the life of the community.

John Goyne married Catherine Letcher in 1848. She was from another long established St Agnes mining family who later branched out into other business interests in the town, one of the family becoming a noted local watch and clock maker.

By the time of the census of 1851, John and Catherine are living at British Row, St Agnes with two daughters, Louisa aged two and Emily aged eleven months. John's occupation here is shown as tin miner, following many generations of miners in the family before him.

This was a time, as we will see in many of the stories in this collection, when Cornwall's economy was in decline. Mines were closing and men were being thrown out of work. No state benefit or unemployment pay in those days.

On the other side of the world, however, prospectors were finding gold and other mineral deposits in vast quantities. Australia was booming and thousands of Cornish mining families were tempted by the prospect of a better life in this fast emerging continent. Free and assisted passages were on offer to miners and other trades and soon the exodus from Cornwall which had begun as a trickle, became a steady stream and then a flood.

So it was that around 1854, John Goyne, by this time the father of four young children, waved his wife and family goodbye as he set out on the SS *Great Britain* for Australia. The SS *Great Britain* was the brainchild of that greatest of the great Victorian engineers, Isambard Kingdom Brunel. She sailed on the trans-Atlantic route for some years, but was making an overall loss for her owners and so she was sold and in 1852 under her new owners, Gibbs Bright & Co., she was refitted as an emigrant carrier.

The company realised the profit potential in carrying men and equipment to Australia and the refit saw a new 500hp Penn engine fitted and a 300ft-long deck house on her upper deck and this, together with other improvements, gave her the capacity to carry as many as 750 migrants in three classes of on-board accommodation to Australia in an average of just sixty days, as opposed to around 100 days normally taken by pure sailing ships at this time. The three-class accommodation allowed for the normal working-class folk as well as their managers, financiers and other professional men to be carried. All the trades and occupations necessary to build and sustain a growing country. Over the next twenty-four years and a total of thirty-two voyages she carried over 15,000 emigrants to Australia and is also credited with carrying the first ever touring English cricket team there in 1861. In 1863 the visiting cricketers aboard were under the captaincy of E.M. Grace, brother to the legendary W.G. Grace. For John Goyne though, as for most of the men on board these sailings, it was to be many years before they saw their loved ones again. Normal practice was for the men to go on ahead, find work and set up a home and send for the families at a later date.

This was indeed no place for families at this time. John was witness to some parts of the Eureka Riots in late 1854. Unrest had been simmering in the area for some time, ever since the discovery of gold in June 1851 at Clunes and in December of the same year at Buninyong in the newly formed colony of Victoria. Up to now these had been quiet, sparsely populated areas where sheep farming was about the only occupation for most folk. The discovery of gold saw a mass immigration from all

Above and opposite: Ruins of tin mines on the cliffs of St Agnes, the home of John Goyne. (Bob Richards)

corners of the world. Many came from Cornwall but many also came from places as diverse as China and the west coast of America where the bubble of the gold rushes there of the late 1840s had all but burst. The government of the region wanted to secure an income for itself for the development of the new colony by means of a licensing system for the miners, but so vast was the influx of gold seekers and so complex the system for the mainly illiterate and often non-English speaking working-class men, that it was completely overwhelmed in its efforts to instil any form of law and order to the proceedings. The system of licensing was introduced but fees required for these were considered too high by the miners and this caused unrest. Generally, the whole system broke down and became unworkable in a very short time, overwhelmed by bureaucracy and sheer weight of numbers. Petitions were presented against government procedures; one such, containing the names of over 5,000 gold diggers from Bendigo, Ballarat, Castlemaine and Alexander stated that:

> Some of the Commissioners appointed to administer the Law of the Gold Fields have on various occasions chained non-possessors of licences to trees and condemned them to hard labour on the roads of the Colony ... a proceeding your petitioners maintain to be contrary to the spirit of the British Law which does not recognise the principle of the Subject being a Criminal because he is indebted to the State.

The colony governor, C.J. le Trobe, had little patience with the protesters and this only served to fuel the flames. Local officials were abused and accused of corruption and unfair practice, in all, a general fever of unrest grew until it exploded into murderous violence at Eureka. Bentley's Hotel was burned down by rioters on 17 October 1854 at the height of a gathering of miners, which had turned into an

ugly riot; several men were later arrested but mostly released for lack of evidence. Other unrest was to follow until a change of government officials, several trials for murder and treason and subsequent pardons seem to have helped quell the situation, but for the newly arrived John Goyne, from the relative quiet of St Agnes, this must have been quite a culture shock and not the sort of thing he would have been promised by the migration agents who went around Cornwall at that time giving talks on the huge benefits to be had of seeking employment in this new colony.

As an indication of the numbers of folk involved here it is estimated that as many as 95,000 migrants came to the area in 1852 alone, mostly living in tented towns along the streams and river banks where most of the gold was to be found. These tented towns would often appear and disappear almost overnight with new gold discoveries in other locations.

Bendigo was the hub of the vast wheel which turned at an ever increasing speed through the 1850s. This place was, as with the whole region, just a quiet country area where sheep roamed freely a decade before. The area was originally known as Bendigo's Creek and the early settlement there had flour and woollen mills, tanneries and a variety of other small production industries which would be associated with any small settlement in a quiet nineteenth-century rural area.

The mining boom certainly changed all that in just a very few short years. Bendigo's Creek, by the way, was named after a man employed on a local farm whose nickname was Bendigo, after the English bare-knuckle prize fighter, William Abednego Thomson (1811-1880). The Australian Bendigo got his nickname for his own style and skill as a bare-knuckle fighter reminiscent of his English namesake who was an interesting character in his own right. He was one of triplets from Nottingham named Shadrach, Meshak and Abednego after the story in the Biblical book of Daniel about the men who emerged from the fiery furnaces of Babylon. William Abednego Thomson was one of twenty-one children. His father died when he was young and he spent some time in the workhouse but by the age of eighteen he was helping with the family budget by fighting for money. He became champion of all England and numbered amongst his 'fans', was Sir Arthur Conan Doyle who penned a verse in his honour. 'Bendigo' Thomson was destined for a life of drunkenness and petty crime, but he was saved by his conversion to religion and joined the Ebenezer Lodge of Templars, giving powerful sermons across the country. He died in 1880 and his headstone reads: 'In Life always brave, fighting like a Lion, in Death like a Lamb, Tranquil in Zion.'

To return, though, to John Goyne. He, too, proved a bit of a lion in Australia. By the year 1858 he had enough money to buy a plot of land at a place called Epsom. He built a small house there and opened a new business, The Stamper Grating Factory. The name says it all. Stampers were the crushing mechanism for the ore from which the gold was extracted, a process very much the same as the old Cornish stamps which crushed the ore before the tin and copper were extracted. The grating was a wire mesh used to trap the gold particles after the stamping process was completed.

By inventing and developing a finer grating, John Goyne was able to produce a product which saved much more gold in the mesh than had ever been possible before, thus increasing the profitability of every single gold digging and stamping operation throughout the area. His invention became an overnight success and within a very short time, orders were being received for his new grating from all over the mining world. W.B. Kimberly in his *Bendigo and Vicinity* history of the area says, 'It would be difficult to estimate how much gold has been saved to the world by means of Mr Goyne's sieves.'

Back in England John's wife and family anxiously waited for news of him with every ship which docked. The 1861 census shows them living at Rosemundy Hill, St Agnes. B2y this time the family is Catherine, thirty-one, shown as a gold miner's wife, with children, Louisa, twelve, Emily, eleven, Catherine, nine and John, seven. Finally in 1866 John felt that the time was right for his family to join him and he was reunited with them after an absence of over ten years. Catherine came first and helped plan a new house. The children followed about a year later and were soon settled into their new home, appropriately named Rosemundy after his own home area in St Agnes.

John and Catherine had three more children in Australia, of which one died as an infant. By the early 1880s, John Goyne had become a wealthy man. Shipments of English sheet iron and steel were arriving constantly at his factory to keep up with the production of his gold sieves. His property at Rosemundy had grown to an estate of some twenty acres, with the house, offices and factory all within its bounds. Six acres were turned over to orchards and the local newspaper of the time likened Rosemundy to, 'a park, with trees, shrubs and gardens almost concealing the house.' A huge bay window faced on to the Bendigo Creek and a small stream meandered through the grounds. Rosemundy was a large house, built of brick with large rooms, marble fireplaces, leaded windows and unusual plaster features. It had a system of servants' bells and was, in time, one of the first houses in Bendigo to be lit by electricity.

The factory often operated twenty-four hours a day to keep up with the demand for its product and on his retirement from the business, one of John Goyne's sons took over and the factory continued to make stamper gratings well into the 1920s. They say that all the best ideas are quite simple and that necessity is the mother of invention and here we have a simple piece of equipment, created and developed by one enterprising Cornishman who saw and met a need. With the profits of his labours, John Goyne was able to create his own little piece of paradise in what had been just a generation before, a place where sheep roamed freely and people were a scarce commodity.

John Goyne died in 1907 at the age of eighty-one years. A service was held at Rosemundy before the funeral cortege of the hearse, drawn by four draped horses and followed by four horse-drawn mourning carriages, left for the cemetery at White Hills.

John Goyne was a man who played no small part in the prosperity of the Bendigo mining area. He made his money from a small and simple invention which helped countless others to recover an incalculable amount of gold which would otherwise have washed away and been lost. He also served the community he lived in, being elected to the Huntly Shire Council and serving there for fifteen years, on two occasions being elected shire president. To this day there is still a Goynes Road and Rosemundy Road in the area where he lived and Rosemundy, the house he named after his childhood home, still stands, perhaps no longer echoing to the sounds of the servants' bells, horses' hooves and the factory next door or even approached along a formal drive with impressive gates and picket fence, but there for all to see as a reminder of this Cornishman whose name is imbedded in the history of the area.

four

Thomas Henry (Harry) Tregonning
A Cornish Miner Evades Justice

On 1 January 1804 in the Parish Church of Gwennap at the heart of Cornwall's mining area a baptism took place of Joseph, son of William and Christian Tregonning. The Tregonning family had roots in this area going back many generations, the family name being amongst the earliest recorded in the surviving parish registers as far back as the 1620s.

They had always been copper miners, working at the nearby Consuls and United mines. Joseph's grandfather had been one of the many miners who were responsible for digging out the great county adit. Begun in 1748 to a plan by John Williams, it eventually helped drain over sixty mines over a vast area from Mawla in the north, right down through the Scorrier and Carharrack mines and on down to Nangiles, Ting Tang and other mines around the Bissoe Valley area. This was an immense feat of engineering which helped sustain even deeper workings for several subsequent mining generations.

However, all was not well with the Cornish copper industry. Around the time that Joseph was born, many of the mines were closing down because of competition from mines in Anglesey, North Wales. Joseph's father walked many miles each day for several years just to find work to help feed his family. Joseph's older brothers were walking to work with him by the age of nine or ten.

Many families left Cornwall altogether and went away to other parts of England to look for work. The Jenkins family, who had been near neighbours of the Tregonnings for many years and who had worked at the same mines, left Cornwall and went to Newcastle in the north of England to mine for coal. Some even went abroad to lands that Joseph and his family had never heard of before. After a few years of hardship and struggle there was a lot of celebration in the area when first United and then Consuls were reopened, thanks to the financial backing of the Williams family from the great house at Scorrier and a man called John Taylor, who was originally from Norwich.

Despite the fact that for the next few years Mr Taylor's mining company provided hundreds of jobs for local families and made money for them and for himself, he was not well liked by all. For nearly twenty years the copper output from Consuls was the greatest of any mine in Cornwall, even larger than the great Dolcoath mine itself. Some of Taylor's Cornish rivals were very jealous of his success and saw to it that when the leases on his mines came up for renewal that these were refused and so, from about 1840 onwards, output from Consuls sank back and depression once more set into the Tregonning family and those around them.

Joseph eventually married Charity Jenkin. Hers was the family who had moved away from Cornwall and found work in the coal mines of Newcastle upon Tyne, where she was born. When Consuls and United were reopened, they, and a lot of others felt the call of their beloved Cornwall and returned home to work again on copper.

Joseph and Charity had ten children, Joseph, Charity, Thomas Henry, Jane, Amelia, John, Sampson, William, Grace, and Mary Ann. Their address at the time was Vogue, St Day. It is believed that Joseph and several of his sons were employed at the once very profitable Wheal Jewel Mine in nearby Carharrack. All too soon, however, there was yet another and even more severe decline in the fortunes of the United

Wheal Coates, St Agnes. One of Cornwall's most productive tin mines, it operated intermittently for over 100 years from 1802. The present buildings on the site date from around 1870 and are today in the care of the National Trust. (Bob Richards)

and Consuls mines. Consuls was taken over by the newly named Clifford Amalgamated Mines in 1857 but even a change of ownership and a change of name could not halt the inevitable decline in its fortunes. From being the world's largest copper mine for many years, with eighty miles of underground workings and nearly twenty engine houses working to help raise and process around 1 million tons of copper, tin and other minerals, the company fell steeply into decline and ceased trading in 1869.

For the second time in little over half a century, families were left without work. Some went to east Cornwall where the mines of Caradon, North Hill and that area were still quite productive. Many were forced again to seek work in other parts of England and Wales but for many, the only solution was a long voyage into the unknown across vast oceans to the New World of the Americas or even further afield to Australia.

And so it was with the Tregonning family who left Cornwall just a few years before the eventual closing of the mines which had been a source of employment for them for so many generations.

In 1865 members of the family took passage on a ship from Liverpool and, just twelve days later set foot on American soil for the first time. They were already making headline news for their onward journey to Central City, Colorado was aboard the first ever stagecoach to make that journey under a new company, 'Butterfield's Overland Dispatch', or, to give it its full title: 'Butterfield's Overland Dispatch to all points in Colorado, Utah, Idaho and Montana Territories. Principle office in Atchison, Kansas: New York office, No. 1 Vesby Street, Astor House.'

Their arrival in Central City, Colorado was reported in *The Rocky Mountain News* of 20 December 1865, where the passenger list includes Sampson Tregoning and Henry Tregoning. Note that the Cornish spelling normally bears a double 'n' in the middle of the name whilst the American spelling is normally with one 'n'.

By the time of the 1870 census of America, more Tregonning family members had crossed the Atlantic Ocean looking for new work and new lives in the thriving mining township of Galena, Jo Davies County, Illinois for here we find in one household, again with a differing spelling interpretation: John Tregonan, thirty-one, with his wife Margaret and their daughters Amelia, aged three and Mary aged just two months along with Charity Tregonan, seventy-one, and Sampson, twenty-seven. The ageing mother of the family, Charity, had lost her husband here in Cornwall and, having no reason to stay, had gone to America with her sons. Sampson was also married but he had left his wife and small children at home in Cornwall whilst he went on ahead to find work and set up a home before sending for the family a little later. This was a common practice amongst emigrating miners. Sadly though, Sampson and his family were never reunited. He, and some of the other Tregonnings, left Illinois to seek work in Colorado and he died either on the journey or shortly after his arrival. His family arrived in America shortly after his death.

Joseph, the eldest son of Joseph and Charity, also emigrated to America. It is not exactly clear when but once in America he met and married Mary Lees, a girl originally from Cork in Ireland. They lived and worked initially around the mining area of Galena, Illinois and later went to Clear Creek, Colorado. Joseph we shall hear more of later, but it is to Thomas Henry Tregonning, known to all as Harry, that we now turn as we continue our story of this Cornish mining family. He had married Emily Harris of Wheal Rose, St Agnes back home in Cornwall and had one daughter, Emily Jane, before leaving for America. Another child, William John, was born in Mineral Point, Wisconsin.

Life was harsh in the mining towns of Colorado at this time. The work was as hard as anything the miners had experience of back home in Cornwall – most basic services were quite primitive, making Cornwall seem in many ways like a paradise. Promises of better lives and better wages and working conditions which had enticed so many to make the journey were still ringing in their ears but for many the sad fact was that these were false promises and the better times had simply failed to materialise. Loved ones were often many thousands of miles away, as in the case of Sampson's family, and it must have been an extremely tough existence. It is easy therefore to imagine that all this, coupled with harsh North American winters, gave rise to severe hardship and tension in the mining towns. Sometimes this overflowed and exploded into violence. The *Weekly Miner* from Georgetown, Clear Creek County, Colorado of 23 January 1873 records:

> Yesterday afternoon witnessed savage and bloody work. Just above Silver Plume, lived Harry Tregoning, a miner with a wife and family. Last summer a difficulty occurred between Tregoning and his wife. He was arrested at the time for ill treatment of his wife but managed to elude the officers of justice. A short time since, Tregoning returned and his wife took him back into her loving arms. Late yesterday afternoon, Tregoning returned it is said, from his work, and shot his wife whom he had pledged his honor to love and support, twice, in a brutal and savage manner, one ball took effect in the right shoulder and the other in the left side. Mrs. Tregoning at last account was still alive but in a very critical condition . . . Tregoning must have attempted his own life as he was tracked to his brother's house by a trail of blood.

Deputy Sheriff Hadley was on the case and 'not withstanding the terrible snowstorm that is raging', the whole neighbourhood was out looking and Thomas Henry (Harry) Tregoning was a wanted man. *The Rocky Mountain News* of the same date records, 'The Carnival of blood continues . . . daily laden with cold blooded murder, shooting affrays and tragic and fiendish crimes of all description.' Not the sort of place for the faint hearted it seems in Georgetown, Colorado in the 1870s. Sadly, *The Daily Miner* recorded within the next two days, 'Mrs. Tregoning died yesterday at her residence 6:00pm.' An inquest was immediately convened which recorded, 'The said Jurors upon oath say deceased came to death by hands of her husband.' And a few days later, 'Harry Tregoning to be tried for the crime of Murder.' Harry Tregonning spent the next few days on the run but *The Weekly Miner* of 30 January reports:

Gwennap Parish Church where Thomas Henry Tregonning was baptised in 1804. Other members of the Tregonning family had been baptised and married in this church for several generations and some are buried in the churchyard. (Bob Richards)

Another view of Gwennap Parish Church where Thomas Henry Tregonning was baptised in 1804. (Bob Richards)

Tregoning in Jail after five days and four nights of awful suffering by cold and hunger and pain of shattered bones in his forearm, by a pistol shot. He went to a miner's cabin last evening in Empire. After being fed and cared for the miner took him to Police.

A reporter from *The Weekly Miner* visited him in jail and although the full account of the visit is not reported, it is said that, 'the Prisoner shed tears and was deeply affected.'

The American process of law took its course over the next few weeks and on Tuesday 8 April 1873 the headline in *The Rocky Mountain News* reads:

Henry Tregoning indicted for Murder . . . We have no comments to make. We have laid the main facts of the awful transaction before the public. After the trial takes place, and the verdict of the jury and the court is rendered, then and not before in our opinion will be the time for incidents and facts concerning a crime that has startled the whole community. First let the majesty of the Law be vindicated.

But Thomas Henry Tregonning was never to stand trial for his alleged crime of murder. *The Georgetown Daily Miner* of Friday 13 June 1873 reports:

Night before last, Jerry O'Brien and Tregoning who were confined in the jail on the charge of assaulting and murder escaped. They were there at midnight, but yesterday morning they were gone and their absence not discovered until breakfast time. The escape was made by cutting a hole through the roof of O'Brien's cell. The ceiling is about 4 inches thick and studded with heavy spikes, 3 inches apart. In spite of these and by the aid of an Auger and Saw, a square hole 18 x 15 inches was made and only one spike met with in cutting.

The prisoners escaped through this hole into the attic, closed up the hole and came down into the south rooms of the building where the doors, being unlocked had no trouble getting out. We think the only assistance given them was the tools. Several men are after them and hope to have them soon.

It was quite apparent that the jail break had not been carried out without assistance from the outside, supplying the auger and saw with which the roof of the cell was cut. The accomplice was Harry's older brother, Joseph. He was a married man with a family and, as well as the trauma of seeing his brother in jail, he was also to suffer a tragic personal loss at this very same time. Just a day after he had helped his brother escape from jail, he lost one of his daughters in a tragic accident, as *The Rocky Mountain News* reports:

Last Sunday at Georgetown a couple of little girls, daughters of Joseph Tregoning, a brother of the wife murderer who escaped from jail on Saturday, were playing upon a log across Clear Creek. While running to and fro upon the log, they lost their balance and fell into the creek, and were swept down in the raging current. One of the children after floating some distance was washed ashore and saved. The other was drowned, the body being carried to a point more than a mile below the foot log.

Little Mary Antoinette Tregonning was just eight years old when she died. Imagine Joseph's state of mind at this time. One night you help your brother to escape from jail, making yourself liable to severe criminal charges and the very next day one of your small daughters is swept away to her death whilst innocently playing on a log across the creek.

Joseph and Harry were now both wanted men.

It is here that the story has an added air of mystery and several possible endings. Joseph and Harry both fled the area, both apparently heading for Canada – whether Harry ever made it to Canada is the subject of some speculation. The Canadian border was over 700 miles to the north through wild and mountainous terrain for two men probably on foot and certainly wanted by the law. No friendly place to hide and no one to trust on the way.

One story is that Harry perished en route. One story is that he made it to Canada where he changed his identity and lived and worked there for the rest of his days. Yet a third story is that by 1885 he was in California, working as a watchman in the New Almaden mining camp there. The truth, probably only Harry and Joseph knew.

As for Joseph, that he made it to Canada is in less doubt. He abandoned his grieving family in Georgetown, Clear Creek County. His wife Mary was left mourning the tragic loss of their eight year-old daughter Mary Antoinette and caring for their other children, Frances Charity, aged ten, Joseph Henry, aged seven and baby Mary Grace, aged just three months. Her life had been churned up by the events of the past few months but it does not seem to have dented her Irish Celtic spirits for more than a brief spell. She lived on to see her three surviving children all marry and bear her grandchildren. The first grandchild, a daughter for Frances Charity, was named Mary Antoinette, in honour of the little girl swept to her death whilst playing at Clear Creek. Mary (Lees) Tregoning died at the age of sixty-four on Christmas Eve 1901 at Silver Plume, Clear Creek County, Colorado.

And Joseph? Yes, he made it to Canada. He too put the past behind him and married again, bigamously as it turns out, to Alice Elizabeth Newlove. They had three children, Joseph, William Henry and Ruth.

Other than Joseph, the family all lived and worked in and around the mining areas of Colorado for this and subsequent generations. Places like Silver Plume, Steamboat Springs and Clear Creek tend to conjure up idyllic settings and the magnificence of the Rocky Mountain foothills but as we have seen, it was not always a peaceful and tranquil place to live.

My most grateful thanks to the descendants of the Tregonnings of Gwennap for their research into the family in Colorado and for their permission to publish the details of these events.

five

The Juleff Family
Crucibles and Stoves

The 1851 census of Redruth shows a family of John Juleff, aged fifty-nine years, born at Copperhouse, Hayle, his wife, Martha and children, Mary Martha and Jabez. John's occupation is given as potter and firebrick manufacturer and the family are living at No. 5 Buller Row, a road name still to be found on modern maps of the town. Next door at No. 6 we find John Juleff, junior, crucible maker aged thirty-two with his wife, Maria and children, John, Sarah, David and Frederick.

The crucibles manufactured by John and his company were much in demand by the mining industry. Small samples of ore were put into crucibles, heated in furnaces to melt the contents and help drive off impurities and the resulting residue of mineral could then be assayed to determine the purity of the metal.

The family name of Juleff, under a variety of spelling interpretations, had its roots many generations before these census records and there were branches of the family in and around Ladock and Probus near Truro as well as further east around St Neot near Liskeard. However, the branch of the family we are looking at here was from the west of Cornwall, in particular the parish of Phillack and the Hayle area.

The crucible business was started as far back as the 1760s by another John Juleff, who, it is believed was the son of Michael and Dorcas, whose maiden name was Carbense. Her family were originally from nearby St Mawgan in Meneage.

The business would eventually pass through several generations of the family from father to son with various other family members having a direct interest. Advertisements of the time showed the business as manufacturing crucibles, muggles, scorifiers and bricks for furnaces.

One family member who ran the business for many years was Michael Juleff, or Julep as it is shown in the parish register at the time of his marriage to Ann Veal in Phillack near Hayle on 9 January 1785. This marriage produced several children including John Juleff in 1792. Michael Juleff died in 1816 and for several years his widow Ann appears to have run the family business in conjunction with a variety of partners, firstly Messrs W. & J. Michell, and later Messrs Penrose & Davey. In 1828 she and the Michells dissolved their partnership for some unknown reason and new partners in Messrs Penrose & Davey were found to steer the company through.

The dissolving of the partnership and the new partners are noted in both the local newspapers of the time and *The London Gazette*, where the company is shown as the Cornwall Crucible Co. Messrs Penrose & Davey had more than a passing interest in the manufacture of crucibles as they were assay masters at Redruth, responsible for the assaying of the minerals brought from the mines.

John Juleff, Ann's son, married Martha Nicholls on 27 January 1812 and he eventually became head of the business which he ran up to the time of his death in 1856. He was buried in the churchyard of St Euny Church on 9 December of that year. His will shows him as 'of the Parish of Redruth in the County of Cornwall, Crucible and Retort Manufacturer'.

After the normal preamble it goes on:

I give and bequeath unto my wife Martha Juleff all my household furniture, household goods, stuff, glass, plate, linen, woollen, clothes and implements of household as her proper goods absolutely.

Also I give unto my said wife all my messuages, dwelling houses, tenements and leasehold premises and all the profits of all my parts or shares in Railway and Gas Works, Machinery Apparatus and Utensils in Trade during her life.

His daughters Ann, wife of John Thomas, and Mary Martha, who later married John Harry, also received a share of his estate. He also set aside a sum of £200, about £12,000 by today's values, to be held in the Cornish Bank, Redruth in the name of his wife Martha and following her death this sum was to be divided between his other children, Michael Broad Juleff, James Juleff and Jabez Juleff. His direct business interests in the crucible and firebrick business he left to Martha and his sons, John and Richard. The will mentions property in Buller Row, cottages at Vauxhall, Redruth and shares in the Cornwall Railway Co. and the Gasworks in Sherborne, Dorset.

Exactly how John Juleff came to have interests in gasworks in Dorset is not entirely clear but it is a valid interest for a man whose company, as well as making crucibles for the mining industry, made retorts, which were used in the gas manufacturing process. It is interesting also to speculate here, did John Juleff benefit from some of the earlier work of gas pioneer and adopted Cornishman William Murdock?

Murdock is remembered as the first man in the country to light his home with gas as far back as 1792, the very year that John Juleff was born. By the time John was starting out on his business ventures, Murdock was long gone from Cornwall and back in London working, but it is quite probable however that John Juleff knew John Reed who established the first Redruth gasworks in 1826, or even James Wynn of Falmouth who set up the first commercial gasworks in that town, and whose son is the subject of another story in this book.

We may never know for certain but he almost certainly provided some of the equipment necessary for their enterprises to flourish, taking shares in their companies and other emerging gas lighting companies and consequently shares in their profits. The Juleff family were not always immune from scandal though. On 14 January 1818, at the Quarter Sessions held in Truro, James Juleff, described as a 'crucible maker of Redruth', was cited by Mary Leane, 'single woman of this Parish', as being the father of her child. The outcome of the case is not recorded but it is likely that James was ordered to pay a sum of maintenance to the child and its mother.

However, the world was fast expanding at this time and another son of John and Martha, Michael Broad Juleff, was tempted by an offer to relocate to the other side of the world in Australia. In the 1840s and 1850s, the Australian government advertised in the Cornish newspapers for suitable men and their families to come to Australia and begin a new life. Many miners were, as we well know, tempted by these offers of free and assisted passages but many businessmen also saw opportunities in this new and fast expanding colony.

Michael's younger brother James had already emigrated to South Australia with his wife Fanny Bond Juleff, formerly Tippet, and by the time Michael made the decision to join him, he and his wife Elizabeth also had six children to consider. Two more children were born to the couple in Australia, one of whom, a son, William died as an infant.

Michael's marriage had taken place in 1837 in the Parish Church of St Euny, Redruth to Elizabeth Gray, the daughter of Richard Gray, innkeeper, and Frances Gray, formerly Trevena. He and Elizabeth had already spent some time out of Cornwall, as the birth places of their children show. Their first two children, Frances Martha and Joseph were born in 1838 and 1839 in Redruth, their next two, Charles James and Samuel were born in Woolwich in 1841 and 1845, then came John, born in London in 1846 and finally, Henry, back in Redruth in 1854, just a few months before the family moved to their new life in Australia.

Michael applied for himself and his family to emigrate to Australia as assisted migrants and he paid £11 for passage under the Assisted Immigrants Act. In modern values this amounts to around £700, the approximate cost of flying one person today from London to Sydney.

After all the decisions had been made and the formalities signed, the family sailed from Plymouth on 21 April 1854 on the *Lady Elgin* and arrived in Sydney on 4 August, some 105 days later. The *Lady Elgin* was a ship of 851 tons and on this journey carried a crew of twenty-six, under her master, Mr D. Irons and her chief officer, Mr Dixon. Her passenger list consisted of 136 males, 116 females and forty-eight children, a total of 300, and it was reported upon her arrival that 'no souls had perished at sea.'

The immigration record shows that Michael Juleff's daughter Frances Martha was a milliner and dressmaker and that his eldest son Joseph was a smith's assistant. The family settled down in Redfern, an inner city area of Sydney where Michael began what was to become his own very successful family business called M.B. Juleff & Son, makers of cooking stoves and colonial ovens.

Records of the area confirm that Juleff Brothers, iron founders, stove manufacturers and general housesmiths, were later located in Regent Street, Redfern and by the time Michael retired and passed on the running of the business to his sons, Joseph and Henry, it was a thriving concern. Awards for the excellence of their products came thick and fast. Many prizes were won for their cooking stoves and other equipment in exhibitions in the 1870s and 1880s.

One of their proudest moments was the winning of an award at the Sydney International Exhibition in 1879. This exhibition, modelled on the famous Crystal Palace Exhibition in London, was housed in a vast purpose-built complex known as the Garden Palace. The huge building took just eight months to complete, partly because of the installation of electric lighting which ensured that work could carry on twenty-four hours a day. It was built mainly of timber which was to be a major contributory factor in its complete destruction by fire just three years after the exhibition in 1882.

The catalogue of the Juleff family company included a range of cooking stoves, very similar to our traditional Cornish range type of stove, and priced from around £2 10s, as well as 'portable washing furnaces', just like the wash boilers of a later generation, but fuelled by coal rather than electricity. A range of ornamental garden seat ends in cast iron was also available from the company and the 'Cornwall Stove Works & Iron Foundry' as it became known was later described as 'one of the most important industries in the city.'

It seems that all of Michael's sons became involved in the business after his retirement to a greater or lesser extent, Joseph and Henry taking a major role but also with Charles and John showing on various records as stovemakers although at the time of his marriage in 1876, John is described as a miner.

Samuel also had an involvement in the business although his main occupation was as a bootmaker who, according to first-hand accounts from his granddaughter, May Johnston, 'made beautiful hand made boots and shoes'. Samuel had also travelled quite widely in both Australia and New Zealand before settling back in Sydney.

Michael Broad Juleff died on 31 October 1896 at No. 84 Morshead Street, Redfern at the age of eighty years. In his forty-two years in Australia he had built up a considerable business empire. He was survived by his widow Elizabeth to whom he had been married for almost sixty years. She lived out her later years with her son Henry and died at the ripe old age of ninety-six years in 1914.

Throughout their years in Australia the family maintained links with their Cornish roots, indeed Henry, born in 1854, just a few months before the family left Cornwall, returned here in 1884 to marry his cousin, Eliza Kate Harry, the daughter of his father's sister, Mary Martha and her husband, John Harry. He returned to Australia just a few weeks after his marriage accompanied by his bride. Henry's main interests lay with the family stove-manufacturing business, but he also took and active interest in other manufacturing matters of direct relevance to his surroundings in Australia.

He was granted a patent for a puddling and gold saving machine in 1894. The technical definition of a puddling machine is, 'A machine used for mixing auriferous clays with water to the proper consistency for the separation of the ore'. In simple terms, a means of helping to separate the gold from the dirt it is found in. Some were small and hand operated, but some were large, looking for all the world like a corn-grinding wheel and operated by a horse walking round and round in circles to crush the clay.

Henry's son, John Michael, became his apprentice and at the Australian National Exhibition in 1905-06, he won the only gold medal awarded in the apprentices' section for cooking stoves. It may seem a bit odd to us in this day and age of electric cookers and all our other 'mod cons' and indeed our massive advertising industry which rams everything down our throats many times a day through our television screens, magazines and newspapers, that these exhibitions were held for such mundane items, but ever since the Industrial Revolution, exhibitions had been held, not all as grand as the Great Exhibition of 1851 in London, but nevertheless extremely important in their day for advertising and selling all sorts of commodities in the days before television and mass media.

If you had a new invention or a new variation of your product, your advertising and your best hope of getting it over to the ordinary folk of the day, was by way of these exhibitions and to win a gold medal was equivalent to a nursery today winning a gold medal at the Chelsea Flower Show. We still do it today – our own Royal Cornwall Show and other agricultural shows around the country, would not exist in their present form were it not for the trade stands offering us goods of every description.

John Michael, or Jack as he was widely known, was the last of the Juleff dynasty to work in the stove industry. He diversified his business interests, adapting the goods he manufactured to suit the changing times and modern needs of the community. He was described in his obituary as, 'surely one of the most versatile men who ever lived in our town who lived to earn the respect and esteem of all who knew him.'

The business, like the long line of the Juleff family, faded slowly away. Henry died in 1938 at the age of eighty-four years, survived by three daughters, Nettie, Kitty and Dorothy, who all lived out their days in the Blue Mountains west of Sydney. None of them married and the last, Dorothy, passed away in 1983.

Relics of the business are still held by family members in Australia, testament to as many as six or seven generations of the Juleff family with their roots here in Cornwall who became pioneers of the new colony of Australia and who have left their mark literally on the streets of Sydney and other Australian cities, where even today it is possible to see that the Juleff name lives on in some of the drain covers and gratings manufactured many years ago in the company's foundry.

There is one other item worthy of note before completing the story of the Juleff family. As has been mentioned, they were related by marriage to the Michell family, a large and very old family from the Gwinear area. Two members of the Michell family had been partners with Ann Juleff in the Redruth business venture in the 1820s. Charles Michell of this same family had married Ellen Juleff and it was Charles who along with John Juleff and Christopher Keiler discovered in 1870 many thousands of pounds worth of gold at a place called Red Surface in the Upper Bingara area. Gold had first been discovered some twenty years previously in this area when it is said that a certain Dr Thompson, accompanied by a man glorifying in the name of Cranky Wyndham, discovered 'bucketfuls of gold' in the area. The inevitable gold rush followed and Messrs Michell, Juleff and Keiler seem to have been some of the lucky few who actually made money out of their finds. As with most gold rushes across the world, very few prospectors actually make much money, most dig for years with little or no success.

My most grateful thanks go to Anne Wilson of Cranbrook, Queensland for information on the Australian side of her Juleff family of stovemakers.

six

John Land Wynn
The Search for the North West Passage

John Land Wynn was born in Falmouth on 13 January 1798. He was baptised at the Parish Church of King Charles the Martyr in the town on 4 May of the same year, the son of James and Grace Wynn. His father was the proprietor of the famous Royal Hotel in Falmouth, which stood just across the road from Fish Strand Quay less than 50yds from the sea. His family had moved to Falmouth from out of county just before John's birth but were already well established in the hotel business in the town. They later bought the lease of the hotel and the name changed to Wynn's Hotel. This was a time when Falmouth was buzzing with shipping activity. Ships of all nations would call here either en route to or from ports all over the world. 'Falmouth for Orders' was the cry. Falmouth's location on the south coast of Cornwall, with a huge natural harbour, made it a very important port.

It was the time of the Napoleonic Wars, which brought the Royal Navy to Falmouth in great numbers. Falmouth also saw many captured ships brought in and their cargoes auctioned. Wynn's Hotel is featured on advertising posters of the day selling all manner of goods 'captured by squadrons of His Majesty's Frigates'. Falmouth was also the first place in England to hear the news of Nelson's death at the Battle of Trafalgar when John Land Wynn was a boy of just seven years old. It is thought by many that Wynn's Hotel supplied the transport which took Lieutenant Lapenotiere of HMS *Pickle* to the Admiralty in London with the news of victory and the death of Nelson.

It was certainly a coaching inn at the time and was advertising daily coaches to Penzance, leaving at 4.00 a.m., going via Helston arriving in Penzance at 9.00 a.m. and leaving for the return trip at 4.00 p.m., arriving back in Falmouth at 9.00 p.m. Five hours to Penzance, a distance of just twenty-five miles and all for just 5d per mile for seating inside the coach and 'outside in proportion'.

As well as daily services to Penzance and other local destinations, coaches would arrive at Wynn's Hotel bringing folk from all over England to the port to take passage to foreign parts. One such was the poet Lord Byron on a stop over before catching the Lisbon Packet boat. The hotel is mentioned in one of his diaries of June 1809. Another reference in the book *Child of Sorrow* reads: 'They met at Wynn's Hotel in Falmouth. In the lower rooms, dozens of men milled about with drinks in hand. Captain Pellew led them up to a dining room on the first floor...' The 1815 *Falmouth Guide* says of the hotel: 'It bids fair to excel, in point of elegance, every other in the West of England.'

In 1817, James Wynn, John's father, installed gas for lighting into the hotel, the first in Falmouth, and this was the beginning of a new business venture which would change his life. Soon he was piping gas for lighting to other properties all over the town. He contracted with the Gilbert Foundry of Totnes in Devon to supply the piping and other necessary materials for the venture. He soon gave up his hotel interests to concentrate wholly on expanding the gas business and the Falmouth Gas Works was opened in 1823 under his ownership. The gas works remained in production on the same site for nearly 150 years. The site is still known to this day by many as the gas works and the remains of some of the huge wooden fenders on the sea wall are still in evidence.

Reginald Watkin Smyth Wynn, 1865-1925,
son of George Murdoch Wynn and grandson
of John Land Wynn.

Kristian Alexander Wynn aged fifteen and Adam Nicholas Wynn aged thirteen. The youngest
generation of the Wynn family, they now live in Westbury near Launcaston, Tasmania and are the
four times great-grandsons of John Land Wayne. (My grateful thanks to Gordon Wynn of North
Turramurra, New South Wales, Australia, great-great-grandson of John Land Wynn, for supplying
these photographs and for permission to reproduce them here)

The *Panorama of Falmouth* guide of 1823 extols the virtues of the new business:

The gas works were first established in this town in March 1819 by Mr Wynn - they were first behind the house but have removed to more commodious premises in Church Street - the circular gasometer is 25 feet in diameter by 16 feet deep and will contain about 9,000 feet cube of gas. The place is much indebted to Mr Wynn for the establishment of these useful works, for this town was the first in the County possessing the advantage even before Plymouth and Devonport.

Exactly what Richard Murdoch over at Redruth thought of this description we are not told for it is he who is credited with lighting the first house in Cornwall with gas, but that is another story.

All this time, John Land Wynn was growing up in Falmouth and what an exciting boyhood it must have been. The son of a hotel proprietor in one of the busiest and most important ports in the whole of England, indeed the whole of the British Empire at the time, it is little or no surprise then that his thoughts turned to a career at sea. He joined the Royal Navy at the age of just twelve on 1 February 1810 as a volunteer, first class.

His first attachment was to HMS *San Juan* at Gibraltar for the Siege of Cadiz. He then transferred to HMS *Elvin* for training, then to the *Sal del Mundo,* a large three-decked 112-gun Spanish prize, captured by the Royal Navy and based in Plymouth as flagship for the commander in chief. John was briefly on HMS *Experiment* and *Owen Glendower* and it was whilst aboard her that he first tasted close naval warfare. The French Cutter *Indomptable* was captured and boarded by a crew from *Owen Glendower* and sailed back into Falmouth. What a day that must have been for a young lad, still only thirteen years of age, to be part of the action which captured the vessel and then sailed it back into his own home town.

His next assignment saw him cross the Atlantic to the Caribbean aboard HMS *Nyaden*, another prize of war, having previously been the Danish ship *Nijaden*.

By the age of fourteen-and-a-half, John was promoted to midshipman and assigned aboard HMS *Nymphe* to the Halifax Station in Nova Scotia during the 1812 war with America. With *Nymphe* and *Bulwark* he saw action attacking shipping in America's New England ports. Peace was declared on Christmas Eve 1814 but even after that, John, now master's mate aboard *Bulwark*, was involved in the somewhat notorious capture of the privateer *Tomahawk* with its crew of eighty-four. *Bulwark* was, at the time, stationed off Boston, with orders to watch the battleship *Independence*. On 22 January 1815, after a chase of ten hours, she captured the *Tomahawk*, under her master Phillip Beeson. She was armed with nine guns, one of them a 24-pounder on a circular carriage, giving the gun much more manoeuvrability during action. On the cessation of hostilities, *Bulwark* sailed to Bermuda, from where she delivered Rear Admiral Griffiths to Halifax, Nova Scotia and then assisted in escorting the transport of some 7,000 British troops back across the Atlantic to Portsmouth. The troops then went on to see action in the Netherlands and *Bulwark* was paid off at Chatham in June 1815.

So by the age of seventeen, John Land Wynn had seen action in European and American waters, had sailed the Atlantic, been promoted and was now, with the end of many of Europe's troubles, about to embark on a phase of his career which would bring him even more excitement.

In 1823, Commander William Edward Parry and Lieutenant George Lyon returned from a two-and-a-half-year expedition with HMS *Hecla* and HMS *Fury* which had set out to discover the legendary North West Passage route to the Orient. It had been Parry's third voyage to these Arctic waters, his second as leader of the expedition. At the same time another Royal Navy ship, HMS *Griper*, was in home waters under Commander Douglas Charles Clavering with Lieutenant John Land Wynn his second in command. Orders soon came from the Admiralty that Clavering and *Griper* should proceed:

… to the coast of Norway about the 70 parallel of Latitude where he is to anchor in such a place as may be most convenient for carrying on observations which Captain Sabine is instructed to make by the Royal Society in London. From thence he is to proceed, for the same purpose, to the Western coast of Spitzbergen in or about the 80 parallel of latitude, and from thence to the Eastern coast of Old Greenland, along which he is to proceed Northerly.

Captain Edward Sabine, of Irish origin but currently of the Royal Artillery was, at the time, one of the leading experts in the field of astronomy. He had been with Parry on his first venture into the Arctic in 1819 and was at the forefront of experimentation to secure a more reliable system of navigation for shipping. Determining longitude was the main navigational problem of the age. Latitude was easily measured but knowing longitude was also essential and bodies such as the Royal Society and many others around the world were working on the problem. This expedition was just one small part of this ongoing work. As well as Sabine, the expedition also took four other scientists to carry out various experiments.

Griper left Deptford on the River Thames in March 1823 and sailed north. The summer was spent taking pendular observations, measuring the slight variations in the earth's magnetic fields at a variety of locations and in other scientific experimentation. Sabine's work was to have a profound effect on young John Wynn. Later he named his second son Sabine in honour of the man with whom he spent that memorable summer of 1823.

The following year, 1824, saw John Wynn preparing for yet another expedition, this time with Commander Parry on yet another quest for the North West Passage. Parry wrote to his brother:

The North West Passage was our next subject. The day before I sent Lord Melville my long letter upon it with which he expressed himself well satisfied, and in which I had stated, after much explanation of the details, that, upon the whole, I considered it well worth another trial.

He went on to say that through the experiences of his previous voyages he now knew at least where not to look for this fabled sea route and that to let others go there and find it would be a waste of the 'expense and labour … of accomplishing this long sought object.'

In a second letter to his brother he wrote, 'Our ships will be commissioned in a few days, I take Hecla as she has some better qualities than Fury … Wynn, who is lately returned in Griper will be my first Lieutenant'.

John Wynn had so impressed his senior officers that he was now to be second in command of the ship which would lead the next expedition to find the fabled North West Passage.

Such was the excitement generated amongst the general public of the day that over 6,000 people signed the visitors' book to tour the two ships whilst they lay at Deptford. A gala day was held on 4 May 1824 and, so confident were they of success that the whole great event was heralded as 'the final resolution to the quest for the North West Passage.'

The ships left Deptford on 8 May and after provisioning downriver, left English waters ten days later. They were accompanied on the first leg of the voyage by a third ship, *William Harris*, a transporter being used to ship some of their supplies across the Atlantic. With Parry's duties as leader of the expedition, it fell to John Wynn to take the everyday command of *Hecla* on the voyage across the Atlantic Ocean. These high latitudes are dangerous waters even today with icebergs and strong winds but back then for a sailing ship with only a masthead lookout and quite primitive navigational aids, they were treacherous in the extreme. Icebergs, often hundreds of feet high above the water and ten times more massive below, were to be found between Greenland and Baffin Island, drifting with wind and current. Compare this to the size of Hecla and Fury, both of which were a mere 100ft in length and weighed just 375 tons. They had both been sturdily built in Hull some ten years previously and were originally built as shore bombardment vessels, capable of firing mortars from their armoury into shore bases. Parry was pleased with their performance on his previous expedition and wrote, 'The ships will combine everything we want, great strength, capacity of hold and fine accommodation for Officers and Men.'

It was not long however before ships and men were tested by the Arctic seas. At just about 60 degrees north, 55 west, they spotted their first iceberg and experienced their first real gale. There is nowhere to run and hide in these waters, no friendly port to make for to see out the gale – 'The wind penetrates everything, nothing can keep it out we shiver and freeze although we are inside.'

The Times of 4 August 1824 meanwhile reported: 'Letters were yesterday received from Captain Parry, from Whale Island, Davis's Strait, crew all well, dated 26 June.' These letters were brought back by the William Harris to Whitby which *The Times* continues, 'left this enterprising Officer on 2nd July.'

This news was already well out of date when received in England, but it was the latest available, no radio or telephone communication back then, just the word of mouth and letters brought back by the supply ship. The reality was that by this time things had taken a turn for the worse.

Parry wrote on 17 July, 'The ice is now beginning to close around us. These obstructions from the quantity, magnitude and closeness of the ice were such as to keep our people almost constantly employed in heaving, warping or sawing through it.'

Eventually they broke through this almost impenetrable barrier into clearer waters and gained a longitude of over 62 degrees west. Parry reported, 'The Hecla was once fairly laid on her broadside by a strain which must inevitably have crushed a vessel of ordinary strength'.

It was now the middle of September, their goal by this time had been Lancaster Sound, at almost 70 degrees north and 80 degrees west, but they were short of this by some way. The sight of land at Cape Warrender and the catching of fresh meat, their first fresh meat in four months since leaving London, cheered their spirits temporarily but by the middle of October, Parry wrote:

> We had the mortification to perceive the sea ahead of us covered with young ice. On reaching it we broke with boats ahead and various other expedients, all ineffectual and obliged us to remain as we were, fairly and immovably beset.

Stuck in the Arctic ice with winter fast approaching, it had always been planned that the expedition should overwinter in these latitudes but not right here, stuck in floating ice, not anchored in any way to land. 'It now appeared' writes Parry, 'high time to determine as to the propriety of still continuing our efforts to push westward, or of returning to England.' Consultations with his officers resulted in the decision to 'pursue our object by all means in our power.' But before they could sit out the winter they had to make some form of landfall. The next few days saw stormy weather, the *Fury* was almost lost.

The crews spent days in trying to lessen the effects of the crushing ice and then the wind changed and they found themselves attached to a body of ice and drifting out of control in the totally wrong direction, eastwards.

Hawsers were run out from *Hecla*, which was still attached to the land ice in an attempt to halt the drift of the *Fury* but these broke and eventually *Fury* was to drift with wind and tide some thirty miles to the east. Only an immense effort on the part of every man aboard got her back and eventually both ships made the relative safety of Port Bowen, their over-wintering post.

Here they remained until July 1825, when the ice finally relented. They sailed westwards again, towards the western shores of Prince Regent Inlet. They were stopped by ice and turned north, hoping for clearer water, but it was not to be. The last days of July saw violent weather, wind and rain batter the two tiny ships. The plan had been for *Hecla* to move south to reconnoitre a clear passage, leaving *Fury* behind. The weather intervened however, and on 31 July, *Fury* was grounded. High tide and the immense efforts of all aboard both ships refloated her but their troubles were far from over. Ice was gathering menacingly all around, like a pack of wolves moving in on a wounded and helpless prey. *Hecla* was forced by the sheer weight and power of the ice onto a beach. *Fury* meanwhile remained afloat but was in fact in more danger. She was bodily lifted by the ice from astern, holing her to such an extent that her pumps could not cope with the inflow of water. Parry wrote, 'The more we considered the state of the *Fury*, the more apparent became the absolute, however unfortunate necessity of heaving her down. She was, in fact, so materially injured as to be very far from seaworthy'. She was moved to a small inlet and all possible weight of stores and equipment removed from her in an attempt to lessen any losses or damage. There followed three whole weeks of constant battle against the elements, trying to repair as best they could a severely damaged ship whilst all the time having an eye to the safety of the *Hecla* which was their only chance of survival if the worst happened to *Fury*.

Parry's decision to remove *Hecla* from the scene and sail for more open waters and to leave *Fury* until the weather improved must have been agonising for him but it was the only possible way of saving his expedition. He wrote, 'As soon as the boats were hoisted up, therefore, and the anchor stowed, the *Hecla*'s head was put to the north-eastward, with a light air off the land, in order to gain an offing before the ice should again set ashore.'

Both crews were now aboard the one ship.

Four days later they returned to the *Fury*. It appeared that the only thing keeping her afloat was a large platform of ice upon which she seemed to sit, cradled in a vice-like grip of death. Parry wrote:

> The first hour's inspection of the Fury's condition too plainly assured me that, exposed as she was and forcibly pressed upon an open and stony beach, her holds full of water, and the damage to her hull to all appearances and in all probability more considerable than before, without any adequate means of hauling her off to seaward, or securing her from the further incursions of ice, every endeavour of ours to get her off, to float her to any known place of safety, would be at once utterly hopeless in itself, and productive of extreme risk to our remaining ship.

The heartbreak of the final decision to abandon *Fury* must have been immense for Parry, for his second in command, John Wynn, and for every last man on both ships. The need now was to pack enough stores on the one remaining ship to serve both crews on the long and desperately depressing journey back to England; their mission to find the fabled North West Passage had once again failed, beaten by the elements. With provisions and crew safely stowed, *Hecla* left Arctic waters heading south and east towards England. The passage was very rough, it was as though the elements were determined to make their own effort to totally destroy what remained of Parry's expedition. It was on 20 October 1825 that *Hecla* arrived back in England at Sheerness. In a little under eighteen months, John Wynn had experienced the most severe extremes of weather, had sailed uncharted and ice-filled waters in a tiny wooden boat and played a large part in successfully navigating some of the most treacherous seas on earth. He had wintered on the ice and played a role in the heroic attempts to preserve the *Fury* from her inevitable fate at the hands of storm and ice. On 30 December 1825, he was to become Commander John Land Wynn, in recognition of his services to the aborted mission to find the North West Passage.

He returned to his home in Falmouth a hero. His father and mother as well as his nine brothers and sisters were there to greet him, along with their respective husbands, wives and children, a host of the good and the great of the area and a certain Elizabeth Symons, a twenty-two-year-old family friend and eldest daughter of the late Robert Symons. Whether planned or not, Elizabeth caught his eye and quite shortly afterwards on 27 May 1827 the couple were married in the Parish Church of St Stythians, just a few miles from Falmouth.

Their first child, a son, was born in 1828 and named Huskisson Curtis Wynn at his baptism in Falmouth on 1 October of that year, honouring the memory of Captain Thomas Huskisson of HMS *Euryalus* who had written to the Admiralty recommending John Wynn as his midshipman and who later added his name to the recommendation that John be promoted to lieutenant. Huskisson had himself been promoted to Commodore of the Barbados Squadron of the Royal Navy but in 1820 had returned from the West Indies in ill health following an outbreak of Yellow Fever.

Their second child was a daughter, Annette Emma, baptised on 12 August 1829, followed by a second son, named Sabine in honour of Captain Edward Sabine with whom John had sailed back in 1823 on his first trip to northern latitudes. A third son, Parry Duchene, came along in 1831, again a name given in honour of a former naval associate, with whom John had experienced the adventure and disappointment of his Arctic excursion.

Not long after this, John took a position on the island of Jersey in the Channel Islands and it was here that his next two children were born, Elizabeth in October 1833 and Louisa Emily in May 1835. Exactly what his official capacity was in the Channel Islands is not clear but after a few years he returned to the mainland and again briefly to Falmouth. His next appointment was to the Packet Service in Portpatrick in Scotland. The Mail Packet Service had been transferred to the Admiralty's new Steam Dept. in 1837 and as such, naval officers were now given control of packet stations, one of these being Portpatrick where a service operated to the northern Irish port of Donaghadee. This was the forerunner of the modern Stranraer to Larne and Greenock to Belfast routes, which were introduced some years later when larger vessels needing larger harbours began to operate the route.

The Portpatrick route had been in use since 1616 when Hugh Montgomerie was granted a licence to operate a ferry between here and Donaghadee. By the time John Wynn was appointed to the position of superintendent the route was operated by steam-powered ships. The first two of these were *Dasher* and *Arrow* which had operated here since 1825. The use of these new, larger steam-powered vessels necessitated the expansion of the harbours at both ends of the route but this was not without its problems. The harbour at Portpatrick in particular was quite small and although it underwent some extension and improvement, in the early days of the steam paddle packets a 180-degree turn was necessary in a confined space to get out of the harbour. At one stage there was a rather primitive device in the harbour whereby a crew member of the incoming vessel would grab a buoy attached to a length of rope and by a system of pulling on ropes and cables and winding of windlasses would assist the vessel in its about turn. Unfortunately this was to prove almost as much of a hindrance as it was a help under some circumstances when wind and tide were not favourable and on one occasion, the rope and winch cable wound themselves around one of the paddle wheels of *Dasher* leaving her totally disabled, drifting onto nearby rocks and, as a consequence, out of action for six months whilst undergoing repairs in Holyhead. In December 1830 she suffered an even worse fate. Strong winds and a heavy sea prevented her from docking at Donaghadee and although the mail was exchanged from a small boat rowed out to the ferry, the passengers were forced to remain on board and return to Portpatrick where again wind and a heavy sea took over, forcing the ferry onto the rocks 200yds from the harbour entrance where she immediately began to break up. Frantic efforts by those on board and those ashore saved the passengers and crew but the ship and mail were lost. Mail bags from the ship and pieces of wreckage were washed ashore as far away as the Isle of Man some three weeks later. A replacement was soon on station, bearing the name *Fury*. Fitting then, perhaps, that the newly appointed Controller of Steam Machinery & Packet Services in 1837 when the Admiralty took over the running of the Packet Service was none other than Edward, now Sir Edward Parry. Doubtless he had some influence in the appointment of his former second in command, John Wynn, to the position of superintendent at Portpatrick, but Parry's initial assessment of Portpatrick seems to sum up the state of the harbour as much as the description of the wreck of *Dasher* a few years before. He commented on arrival that, 'Upon the whole, I could scarcely have imagined a more wretched harbour for Packets if I had not seen Portpatrick.'

A rail link was later introduced to the harbour at Portpatrick but its days as a ferry terminal were numbered. The mail was transferred to the Greenock to Belfast route by 1849 and, despite the coming of the railway to both ends of the route, it closed to passengers in 1891.

Sadly, John Wynn's days at Portpatrick were also cut short. His youngest son, George Murdoch Wynn, was born there in 1842 but soon afterwards on 30 April 1844, John Land Wynn died at the young age of forty-six years. He is buried in the churchyard at Donaghadee on the Irish side of the ferry route from Portpatrick. The church is within sight of the harbour and the sea, a fitting place for this mariner to be laid to rest. The inscription on his headstone reads:

In memory of John Land Wynn Esq. Commander in the Royal Navy, Superintendent of Her Majesty's Packet Service at Portpatrick, where he died on the 30 day of April 1844, aged 46 years leaving a widow and nine children to deplore his loss.

Underneath is a short verse:

I ascend to my Father and your Father, to my God and your God.

His death was noted in the local press here in Cornwall where the *Falmouth Packet and Cornish Herald* notes that, 'he leaves a widow and nine children to regret the irreparable loss of an affectionate husband and indulgent father.'

John Land Wynn's contribution to Arctic exploration was posthumously remembered by the award in 1857 of the Arctic Medal, an octagonal silver medal surmounted by a five-pointed star and ring with a watered white ribbon attached. Only certain specified Arctic expeditions were acknowledged by this honour and John's expedition both with Captain Clavering aboard *Griper* and his later trip with Commander Parry aboard *Hecla* qualified him for the honour.

Elizabeth and the children did not stay long in Scotland after his death. Within a few years she was living in London and later moved to East Budleigh in Devon. The family grew and most of them married. Although not all have been traced, Annette married a shipping clerk by the name of Thomas Perman and settled in London, her sister Elizabeth became a school governess and, as far as can be ascertained, never married. George, the youngest son, took to the sea. He sailed the route from England to Australia and settled there in 1864 where he became a captain operating coastal vessels. He married there to the daughter of a friend of his father and descendants of that family still live in Australia.

The North West Passage remained the quest of marine explorers for many years after the death of John Wynn. It was not until 1905, nearly 100 years after John Land Wynn was born, that Roald Amundsen finally led a successful expedition through these fabled waters. Today and a further 100 years or so later, we hear that because of global warming there are new prospects that this 'shortcut' from the Atlantic to the Pacific may one day soon be a commercial route. It seems that Mother Nature may yet have the final word in this story.

It is to Gordon Wynn, a direct descendent, that I am deeply indebted for most of the information relating to the career of John Land Wynn, the boy from Falmouth.

seven

Richard Luke Kitto
Miner of Gwennap

Thomas Kitto married Mary Ann Middleton, a family name we shall see again later, on 24 April 1798 in the Parish Church of St Euny, Redruth. Their first child, Thomas, was baptised in the same church on 5 August 1798, just four months after his parents' marriage.

It was quite a normal fact amongst families of the time that the imminent arrival of a child hastened the parents' step to the altar. There followed Elizabeth, 9 March 1800; Mary Ann 20 June 1802; Hannah, 29 April 1804; William, 20 April 1806; James Henry, 28 February 1808; John, 13 July 1809; and Mary Ann, 9 May 1811.

Two daughters with the same name is an indication that the elder sibling died young and the name was given to a later daughter. The first Mary Ann was buried on 3 November 1804. Eight children in total – perhaps six of them grew to adulthood, typical of the times when poor diet, poor living conditions and a lack of medical provision all contributed to a harsh life. These were generally harsh times in Cornish mining communities. Although new steam-powered pumping engines had been introduced into Cornwall's mines as long ago as 1720 and their use had meant an upsurge in production with deeper, more profitable mining than ever before now possible, the increased prosperity was to last only a couple of generations.

Our next generation of the Kitto family sees James Henry marry Christian Luke in Gwennap Parish Church on 20 February 1830. The family name of Luke appears amongst the earliest surviving parish registers of Gwennap and also in the neighbouring great mining parish of St Agnes just to the north.

At the time of the 1841 census we find the family living at Treskerby just outside Redruth with: James Kitto, thirty, miner; Christian Kitto, thirty; John Kitto, nine; Thomas Kitto, seven; Richard Kitto, five; and James Kitto, three.

Remember here that the 1841 census is notoriously inaccurate with the age of many adults and indeed many children. This is through nothing other than the lack of knowledge of those folk being enumerated. It is not only found in Cornwall but was a recognised fact all over the country and the census enumerators were instructed to be accurate where possible with age, otherwise be accurate to the nearest five years, hence the predominance of folk on this census with '5' or '0' on their age. Remembering age and birthdays was far less important than earning a living to feed the family.

Richard Kitto, the third son of the family, was baptised in Redruth on 16 March 1837 and it is interesting to note that he was not the only bearer of that name to make his mark on nineteenth-century Cornwall. Another Richard Kitto, a native of Breage parish, received a commendation from the King of Norway in 1847 for his gallant services in saving lives from the wreck of the Norwegian Schooner *Elizabeth* which was wrecked off Porthleven. He became a successful boat builder in Porthleven, specialising in fishing boats and the business ran in the family for several generations.

By the time of the census of 1851 we find our Kitto family still at Treskerby and increased by four more children. We now have: James H. Kitto, forty-three, tin and copper mine agent; Christian, forty-two, wife; John L., nineteen, tin and copper miner; Thomas L., seventeen, mine blacksmith; Richard, fourteen, scholar; James C.M., twelve, tin dresser; Mary A.M., nine, scholar; Francis M., six, scholar; Elizabeth M., four, scholar; and Kitty L., one.

Of note here is that James has risen from the normal 'miner' of 1841 to 'mine agent' by 1851, a promotion and a position of better standing in the community. Interesting too that although James at the age of twelve is out working, which was quite normal for a child of his age at the time, his older brother Richard is still a scholar. This is the first sign that Richard Kitto was receiving an education which would lead on to greater things in his later life. Nothing is known about exactly where he received his education but it was quite probably at the nearby Trevarth School, an educational establishment set up in 1835 by wealthy mine owners and others wishing to see their children educated to a good standard. This was still a time before education was generally free and available to all, but there were several schools and places of learning available in the area. For example, Truro Grammar School had been running since 1549 and a new grammar school in Falmouth opened in the 1824 and there were others associated with local churches and run by benevolent folk from their own homes. Sadly James Henry, the father of the family, died in 1854 at the age of forty-six years. This to us is a very young age but for a Cornish miner of the time, it was not uncommon to die before the age of fifty. The dreaded 'miner's lung' accounted for many of them. This was a disease brought on by years of inhaling dust and other impurities in the mines; it gradually clogged up the lungs, making breathing difficult and ultimately impossible. Today we would call it *Pneumoconiosis* and modern mines have extractors and other precautions against it but at the time of James Henry Kitto, sadly, it was an awful and painful fate suffered by thousands.

So here we find Christian Kitto, a widow in her mid-forties with a family where four or five are still dependant on her and the older children to keep them. At the time of his father's death, Richard was eighteen years of age. By now he was earning a living and contributing to the family income. About now there is also a very interesting entry in the baptism register of St Euny Church, Redruth. A note is appended to Richard's original 1837 baptism entry which reads, 'Luke added 20 October 1855 by J.W.H.' Richard thus became Richard Luke Kitto, taking his mother's maiden name as a second forename. Later he was to become known as Richard Luke Middleton Kitto, having also added his grandmother's maiden name to his own given name.

'J.W.H.' in this entry was J.W. Hawkesley, one time Curate of Illogan, later Rector of Redruth and subsequently Rector of Turvey, Bedfordshire. Why these additions are made we have no explanation but the addition of 'Luke' would seem to be an acknowledgement of his family ties at a time when he was just about to set out on a journey which would see him leave Cornwall for the other side of the world.

By 1857, Richard Kitto is to be found living and working in Bendigo in Australia. This was an area which saw its own gold rush in the 1850s when thousands of foreign migrants from places as diverse as Cornwall and China flocked here looking to make their fortune.

Like all gold rushes, this one too was all but over in a very few years. Although some alluvial gold mining carried on, the main mining emphasis turned to quartz in and around places like Fryerstown where Richard Kitto found himself deeply involved with the early development of the industry.

Initially it appears that he combined some teaching with his mining enterprises but soon mining took over his life. He became a mine manager and his education and knowledge helped secure the financial backing for several mines in the Bendigo area. Within about ten years of his arrival in southern Australia he was elected to office in the Legislative Assembly of the State of Victoria. He held this position only briefly up to 1871 due to the pressures of his ever increasing mining and other enterprises but during that time he was instrumental in bringing about many improvements to the well-being of the population of the area. One of these was a water supply to the town of Fryerstown, from the Crocodile Reservoir, parts of which are still in use to this day. He also persuaded the

Ministry of Mines that there was an urgent need for an explosives store closer to the ever expanding quartz mines of Fryerstown as the nearest at the time was about seven miles away in Castlemaine. This was built at the end of the wonderfully named Nuggety Gully Road, just outside the town, far enough for safety in case of accident but close enough for convenience. He was also instrumental in improving harbour and shipping facilities at Morrison's Haven, a vital port for the area and he helped to finance and develop rail links across the mining regions of Victoria.

During this time of fast expansion in his business empire he never forgot his native Cornwall. The late 1860s and early 1870s saw severe depression in Cornwall's mining industry causing hardship for mining families. This hardship also rubbed off onto other trades and professions because if the miners had no money, then they could not purchase the food grown by the farmers, or employ the services of other tradespeople so everyone suffered and the poverty chain consequently entangled the whole county. Funds were set up in the thriving mining areas around Bendigo, Ballarat and Castlemaine as well as other Cornish communities around the world to help alleviate the suffering of Cornish miners. Many of the miners of these areas were, of course, originally from Cornwall and this was their way of helping out their folk back home.

Richard Kitto played a major part in helping to alleviate the suffering in Cornwall. He came home and visited the county, giving talks to miners and others about the benefits and opportunities available in the mining regions of Victoria. He personally assisted in making the necessary arrangements for the passage for hundreds of Cornish folk to the other side of the world. His benevolence even extended as far as building streets of houses in the mining areas for his new workers from Cornwall.

His return to Victoria was, however, quite short-lived. In 1874 his most ambitious venture, the Duke of Cornwall mine closed down. The only remaining sign of this once great mine is the towering engine house still to be seen near Fryerstown, like so many in Cornwall, silent reminders of a bygone age and industry. Richard Kitto was then offered a very lucrative position with the Preston Pans Iron & Coal Mining Co. in Scotland. His reported salary is given as £1,400, the equivalent today of over £80,000 a year. Sadly however, Richard Luke Middleton Kitto, as his father before him, did not reach his fiftieth year. He died on his forty-fourth birthday in 1880 at his home in Scotland. He left behind a widow and ten children to mourn his sudden passing but he also left behind a huge legacy to mining communities as far apart as Gwennap in Cornwall and Victoria in Australia.

eight

Delabole to Pennsylvania
A Story of Slate

We hear a lot about Cornish tin and copper miners going all over the world to seek new jobs and new lives when our mines here closed during the nineteenth century and the county suffered a severe decline in its overall fortunes, but what of others?

Many farmers and other tradesmen are also to be found among the lists of emigrants and our slate quarrying men from the Delabole and Tintagel areas of North Cornwall were by no means exempt from the overall slump in the nineteenth-century Cornish economy. Many of the slate quarries of the Delabole area of north Cornwall suffered a similar fate to our tin and copper mines in the nineteenth century, throwing men out of work and leading to migration of workers to other parts of Britain and further afield.

One such man was William Chapman. He was born in north Cornwall and worked in the slate quarries around Delabole as a young man but when work became harder to find in that area he went to North Wales where he worked in the slate quarries of Penrhyn. But his sense of adventure was to get the better of him and he set sail in 1842 from Caernarfon bound for New York aboard the barque *Hindoo* under Captain Richard Hughes. Of the 230 who set out, two died on the voyage but the others were safely delivered to New York on 28 May of that year.

William made his way to Pennsylvania where he began work in the local slate quarries. Some say that he was the first to discover and quarry slate in this area, but history shows that slate had been quarried here in a small way for perhaps 100 years before William Chapman's time. Whatever the true story, he can certainly be credited with being responsible for a vast expansion in the slate industry of Pennsylvania. Within a few years of his arrival he had saved enough money to purchase some land and open his own slate quarry. He recruited men from the local community but these were mainly farming folk with little or no experience of quarrying or of the skill Chapman needed to turn the raw slate into the quality roofing material he had known in Cornwall. As a result, William Chapman recruited men direct from the Delabole area who had generations of slate quarrying skills behind them.

Quarries were opened in Bangor in 1853 and in Pen Argyl in 1854 and others were to follow, almost entirely manned by ex-Cornish quarrying men from north Cornwall.

Names on the 1866 tax rolls of the Slate Belt include many of Cornish descent such as: Bennett, Bray, Bonney, Davey, Gist, Heard, Hockin, Jackson, Kellow, Lane, Marshall, Masters, Miller, Parsons, Paul and Williams. As was the case with the tin miners the men often arrived alone and worked until they had enough resources to send for their families.

The 1850s through to the 1870s were the height of immigration for the Cornish to the Pennsylvania Slate Belt. Prior to 1872 most of them settled in Bangor. After that time the Cornish were to settle in East Bangor and Pen Argyl. By 1900 the census shows 42 per cent of the names recorded in East Bangor to be of Cornish descent. Between 1880 and 1900 the total number of Cornish households in the Slate Belt increased from 441 to 1,721.

Among the hundreds of families who made this journey were the Parsons family and the Bray family and their stories are typical of many who went to the Slate Belt to work. They had lived in and around the parishes of north Cornwall for many generations but when work became harder to find, the attractions of a better life across the vast Atlantic Ocean lured them away. One story told to me recently of these early quarrying men concerns the Parsons family of Delabole. This family's history has been traced as far back as 1689 in and around Tintagel and Davidstow. At the age of ninety-three, W. Roslyn Parsons, a direct descendant of John B. Parsons of Cornwall, had this to say about his journey with his family sometime in the 1880s:

My Dad's Uncle Jack did very well in America and a few years later he was employed as a Superintendent over several slate quarries in the Bangor area, so he wrote to Dad and offered him to come to work in one of the slate quarries he had charge of. We sailed from the port of Liverpool, or it could have been Southampton, on the steamship 'SS Philadelphia' and docked at Ellis Island, New York. At that time the ships were not as fast as today. I think it was a two or three week journey.

I had a ball and I was the only one of the six children who did not get sea sick.

Dad and Mom brought four or five pairs of Grooter strain racing pigeons. It cost nothing to bring them on the ship at that time. He had to care for them in every way and keep them in our cabin.

Life was a little rough for a while as it was not easy coming to a new country with six children and then two more here later, but it was not long before Mother and Dad could see things were looking good. When we went to school at first the children got a laugh out of the way we spoke the English language as we had that Cornish brogue or accent, but all in all we did OK before very long.

An outline of some of the Bray family who were originally from Treknow near Tintagel also illustrates how the Cornish went from being slaters to owners of their own businesses and in later generations on to university to become professional men.

Joseph Bray was born in Cornwall in 1835; his family had also been in this area for many generations. He emigrated in 1856 and settled in East Bangor, Northampton County, Pennsylvania, where he was one of the pioneers in the slate industry. He was a good businessman and in addition to being a slate pioneer he was one of the organisers and founders of the Methodist Episcopal Church at East Bangor. He married Louise Preston who was also of English parentage and birth. They were the parents of four children: William; Anna Mary; Joshua and Milford. William Bray, eldest son of Joseph and Louise was born in Champmansville, Pennsylvania, on 1 August 1858. The town was named after William Chapman, the original pioneer of the Slate Belt. Seven years later his parents moved to East Bangor, where William attended the public school and obtained his education. He began working in the slate quarries and for many years he continued as an employee. In 1886 he began operating in association with his father, and in 1888 was elected treasurer and superintendent of the East Bangor Consolidated Slate Co., a position which he held for thirty years. In 1906 he was one of the organisers of the Jackson Bangor Slate Co. of Pen Argyl, Pennsylvania, the largest slate corporation in the United States. In that corporation he was a director and vice-president. In 1910 William Bray organised the Albion Bangor Slate Co. of Wind Gap, Pennsylvania and was director and vice president. He formed an association with C.M. Miller in 1912 and purchased the Alpha Slate Co. of Bangor, and in 1914 he organised the Banner Slate Co. of Danielsville, in company with gentlemen from Scranton, Pennsylvania. He was a director and president of that company. He was a director of the Bangor and Portland Traction Co., director of the Northampton Traction Co. and of the Delaware Valley Railway, running from Stroudsburg to Bushkill, Pennsylvania. His large slate interests were carried on alongside another large and prosperous business, consisting of general merchandise and a coal department incorporated under the name of Bray Bros & Rasely.

William Bray was a member of the Methodist Episcopal Church of East Bangor, serving as superintendent of the Sunday school for over thirty years, succeeding his father, who was one of its founders. He married Mary Ellen Ackerman, daughter of Isaac and Catherine (Myers) Ackerman. They became the parents of four children: R. Foster Bray was born in 1884 and became a selling agent for the Paige automobile, in Philadelphia; Anna Mary Bray married Chest Booth of Shrewsbury, Pennsylvania, manufacturer of piano stools and benches; Joseph Truman Bray was born in 1887 and died in December, 1918, being then connected with the Quartermaster's Dept of the Students of Wesleyan University; and William P. Bray, born in 1891, later became a graduate of Hackettstown Centenary Institute, New Jersey, Wesleyan University, Middletown, Connecticut and the law department of the University of Pennsylvania. He practiced law in Bangor.

Another Bray descendant became a financial broker and another also went into the financial world, founding a savings and loan company.

They were quite a variety of folk who all made very good lives for themselves and who were all descended from Cornish slate quarrying families. At one time there were eleven quarries within Bangor borough limits and numerous others in the surrounding towns of the Pennsylvania Slate Belt. None of them are operational today but the area has not forgotten its founding fathers. The Slate Belt Heritage Center that occupies the former town hall building in Bangor preserves the local history and heritage of the Slate Belt region.

A slate-industry room tells the story of the grand days of the slate quarries and a Cornish Heritage room illustrates the homely comforts of a typical Cornish kitchen so familiar to many of us from our childhood days. A mural covers the entire wall of the staircase leading to the second floor with a depiction of the history of Bangor from its beginnings to the end of the twentieth century.

Northampton County, Pennsylvania currently has a population of around 280,000, quite a high proportion of whom can still trace their ancestry to Cornwall and also to Wales. Some of the place names there are reminders of some of the families who settled there in those early days and the places they came from. Bangor is an obvious one, named after the town in North Wales where a lot of the slate men came from. Names like Ackermanville, Rasley Town, Millers and Chapman are all from families we have met in this short story of the area. And yes, of course, there is also a place named Delabole. It is only a small dot on a large map, but it is a constant reminder of the heritage of the area.

I am indebted to Doris Parsons Miller of Reading, Pennsylvania for much of the information on the American side of this story. She is a direct descendant of both the Parsons and the Bray families of north Cornwall and is herself a former freelance artist with credits in several *Who's Who* editions, including the *Who's Who of American Women*. She was also mentioned in recent years as a Notable American of the Bicentennial Era.

nine

The Story of Sammy Wroath
High Flyer from Newlyn

On the north-eastern slopes of Bodmin Moor lie the parishes of Tresmeer and Treneglos. These are very ancient places with evidence of settlement by man from the earliest times, several millennia before the time of Christ. The site of the present-day church may well have been a place of gathering and worship for much of that time. It is situated at the end of a winding uphill climb through leafy Cornish lanes in a circular churchyard, often evidence of a much older religious site. Its first official mention is in the pages of the Domesday Survey of 1068. It was for several centuries after that under the domain of the Priory of Tywardreath up to the Dissolution of the Monasteries by Henry VIII.

Treneglos Church in particular has undergone much change since that time, including a new tower as recently as about 1880 as the old tower was crumbling and dangerous. Its four bells dating from 1712 were rehung in the new tower. The surviving parish registers of baptism, marriage and burial are available from the late seventeenth century, with a few gaps where they have been lost over time, faded away or in other ways deteriorated as a result of being kept in often damp churches. It is to these records though that we turn for our first mention of the Wroath family name. It is a name which had been in the north Cornwall area even before this time. In Tintagel, on the coast on the other side of Bodmin Moor for example, there is a marriage of John Wroth to Grace Battyn as early as 1603 and in nearby St Teath, Grace Wroth married Thomas Nicholl in 1626. Lantelgos by Camelford also has early mentions of the name, with the expected spelling interpretations of the time. This was, remember, a time well before most folk had any formal education and learning to read and write was a very poor second to earning a living and so families relied on the churchmen of the time to make the entries in the baptism, marriage and burial registers and often their interpretations of spelling of names varied. This is an accepted part of any family history research from this era.

By the 1740s we find in Tresmeer the baptism of John, son of John and Mary Wroath, and Degory, son of John and Mary two years later. Details on these old parish registers are quite sparse and so it is not always possible to be certain of a direct family line down the years but by research and process of elimination it is very possible to follow a line which is as accurate as surviving detail will allow.

In 1773 there is a marriage here between Digory Wroath and Honour Willcock. The Curate has published two sets of banns for this marriage, one with his name first and another with her name first, quite unusual to find two sets of marriage banns in the same parish but the curate, James Rouse, was obviously making sure he got it just right. He had plenty of experience of such matters and who are we to question the ways of a man who served as curate for this church for some fifty years from 1771?

This marriage, like most of its time, produced several children. A total of nine have been found between 1776 and 1798 baptised in Tresmeer and in neighbouring Treneglos, in the old round granite font, which is still there with its large claw feet. One of the sons of the marriage was Thomas and he, together with his brothers Digory and John, made the move from north-east Cornwall to Truro, about fifty miles to the west, at some stage in their youth.

Truro was then a thriving port, much more important than Falmouth and it held the Assay Office for the rich tin and copper mines inland in the great mining parishes of Gwennap and Kenwyn. It also had a vibrant market and commercial heart. This was a time of exploration and discovery, the world was suddenly hearing the names of new countries and places like Africa were being explored and exploited. One Truro boy of this era was the explorer Richard Lander who, together with his brother John made trips to the west coast of Africa, discovering a sea route from the interior of that dark continent to the ocean along the River Niger. Lander died in Africa just around his thirtieth birthday but the legacy of his discoveries lived on and others followed his lead into Africa and began to open up and develop the continent and its hidden wealth.

Meanwhile, back in Truro the Wroath family were becoming quite prominent citizens in their own ways. Family members plied their trades in the ever-expanding Truro of early Victorian years; they were whitesmiths, wheelwrights and blacksmiths, another ran a hostelry, the Coach & Horses in King Street and another went further west to Penzance where he became a fisherman out of Newlyn, an important fishing port then as now.

The census of 1851 shows Digory Wroath, a name handed down through several generations of the family, born in Truro and now aged eighteen and a fisherman aboard the vessel *Conqueror of Newlyn*, with her master, William Payne, a Newlyn man through and through with much fishing experience to his family name. In fact the census of 1841 shows at least four Payne families in and around Green Street, Newlyn, three as fishermen with one as a shipwright, so the sea was firmly in the family blood.

Digory Wroath married into the Payne family. He married Elizabeth Deeble Payne, the daughter of his employer William and his wife Patience and, by the time of the next census in 1861, he had four children of his own, including Samuel Deeble Wroath, born in 1860. Digory's wife Elizabeth died at the age of just forty-six years in 1880. Digory remarried in 1883 to a widow, Mary Boase, whose maiden name was Fraggean, another well-known Newlyn family name. He lived out the rest of his days in Newlyn and died in 1913 at the age of eighty years. Samuel Deeble Wroath, his son, married Edith Cattran quite late in life, in 1907.

As with the names of Payne and Fraggean, and their various spelling interpretations, the name of Cattran is one where you would be hard pressed to find many born out of sight of St Michael's Mount. Some family names seem to spread far and wide across the county but some seem to stay for many generations in the same area. The Cattran family of Paul and Penzance were mostly associated with the sea, and the family branch from nearby Ludgvan parish were by contrast miners, both true Cornish occupations of the time.

The marriage of Samuel and Edith was blessed with a son, named Samuel after his father, born on Boxing Day 1908 at 26 Parc Saundry, Madron, near Penzance. Samuel's early life was spent in this area but in his youth, whether because his parents had died or because he showed a particular promise is not clear, he went away to the London area to live with family members there. Later he was to join the RAF. Here his career literally took off. By the middle of the 1930s it was clear that Europe was gearing up for another major war. New armaments were being produced and tested and one of these was an aircraft known originally as the Fury Monoplane but much better remembered by its later name of the Hurricane. It first flew in 1935 and in February 1936 the prototype was handed over to the Air Ministry Aeroplane and Armament Experimental Establishment at Martelsham Heath in Suffolk for further testing and evaluation. A lot of this early flying was carried out by the then sergeant, Sammy Wroath. Initially these flights took place with no arms fitted to the aircraft but after successful initial test flying, eight Browning machine guns were fitted to the aircraft in August 1936. The original prototype proved so successful that the aircraft went into full production soon afterwards and it went on to play a vital role in the Second World War, in the Battle of Britain campaign and in many other airborne battles.

Sammy's career also went from strength to strength. After the initial success of the Hurricane it became the star of a 1938 film entitled *Test Pilot* and starring such big names of the era as Clark Gable, Mryna Loy, Spencer Tracey and Lionel Barrymore. Clark Gable played the test pilot of the title and it was Sammy Wroath who did the flying sequences for the film.

By 1938, Sammy was commissioned in the RAF and served throughout the war years. In 1946 he was promoted to wing commander and on 1 January 1954, the boy from the lowly fishing family in Newlyn was promoted to group captain. He became the first ever commandant of the Empire Test Pilot School and retired from the RAF in 1957 with CBE, DFC and Bar to his name. Among his other honours was to be elected as an honorary fellow of the Society of Experimental Test Pilots.

Other members of the Wroath family also served their country in times of war and at least two of them paid the ultimate sacrifice. Able Seaman William Wroath of the Mercantile Marine was lost at sea on active service aboard the SS *Coath* on 13 December 1916 at the age of just thirty-three years. He was the son of William and Annie Wroath and the husband of Mary Wroath (formerly Polglans) of Vanguard House, Mousehole, Penzance. His name is listed on the Tower Hill Memorial, London and on Mousehole Methodist Church War Memorial. The SS *Coath* was sunk by a mine in the English Channel. Sixteen of the crew, including the master, died.

The Second World War claimed another member of the west Cornwall Wroath family from its next generation. Lance Corporal Richard Wroath is remembered with honour amongst the Commonwealth War Dead on the Memorial at Moascar in Egypt. He died in April 1944 whilst serving with 203 Provost Co. of the Corps of Military Police. He was the son of Richard Pentreath Wroath and his wife Edith of Mousehole. From humble beginnings high on the moors of central Cornwall to the sands of the Egyptian desert is a long way, but the two are linked by this one family and their service to their country in time of need.

ten

John H. Jeffery
Cornwall to Keweenaw

No collection of stories of Cornish pioneers and their exploits would be complete without mention of the Keweenaw Peninsula, part of the Upper Peninsula of Michigan, USA and an area bordering on the Great Lakes. This was a favoured destination for many thousands of Cornish miners and their families together with a wide cross-section of the other trades and occupations necessary to sustain a thriving community. The Keweenaw Peninsula is famous for its copper. As here in Cornwall, there is evidence to show that nineteenth-century miners were by no means the first to exploit this valuable mineral wealth. Copper originating from the Great Lakes area has been identified in tools used by ancient civilisations across the whole of North and South America. It was not, however, until events in 1842 that the real copper boom began. A treaty was signed on 4 October of that year, handing over lands occupied for countless generations by the Chippewa Indians to the United States Government. Under the terms of this treaty the native tribes would receive payment for their lands, but would also be subject to removal at the whim and pleasure of the United States president, particularly if copper was found on these lands. The way was open for the prospectors to move in and so, several years before the famed California Gold Rush of 1849, there was a copper rush in this northern outpost of the United States. All travel was by boat as the area was densely forested. Soon townships such as Copper Harbour, Eagle Harbour and Ontonagon were springing up. The early years were as chaotic as anything seen later in California, most of the initial investors and prospectors did not make the fortunes they hoped for and by the end of the 1840s only a few of the companies who had originally speculated in the area were still in business. However, the scene was set and mining on an organised and large scale was now becoming a reality.

Our story begins with a mining theme but as we unfold the stories of those who were born here in Cornwall and those who were subsequently born in America in the next generation, we shall see that not all those who initially went for the mining remained in that line of work. The other natural resource of the Great Lakes area is timber, or lumber as it is known in those parts and, as we shall see, there was also considerable Cornish influence in the lumber trade.

On 13 August 1848 there took place in the register office at Liskeard a marriage between Simon Jeffery and Elizabeth Gribble Williams. The marriage certificate tells us that his father was John Jeffery, deceased and her father was Colon Williams. As with most records of this era, the spelling of some names varies and where this occurs, they have been reproduced here as they are found in various original documents. By the time of the 1851 census we find the Jeffery family living at Barn Street, Liskeard. Simon Jeffery is shown as a lead miner aged twenty-five with wife, Elizabeth, twenty-two, born in Calstock and two children, John Henry aged two with a given birth place of Callington and Mary Elizabeth aged seven months, born in Liskeard. Simon's place of birth on this census is given as St Mewan, which is just outside the town of St Austell and here in the Wesleyan Methodist baptism register we find an entry which reads, 'Simon the son of John Jeffery and Elizabeth his wife of St Ewe born 16 December 1825 and baptised on 13 January 1826 by Edward Millward.' John and Elizabeth had been married just a few months before Simon was born.

The 1841 census has the family living at Tywardreath, a few miles east of St Austell, and family events in a short period of twenty-five years or so shows that they had moved several times. The main reason, in fact the only reason for most folk for moving from one location to another at this time, was in search of work.

The locations of St Ewe, St Mewan, Tywardreath, Callington and Liskeard were all mining areas and in common with many other families it seems that the Jeffery family were moving around Cornwall trying to find work in an ever deteriorating situation with mines closing and work becoming harder to find.

Similarly the Williams family; although it is not possible from current research to be certain, it appears that this family were originally from the Gwennap area of west Cornwall and that they moved east to Calstock on the River Tamar sometime around the end of the eighteenth century. A lack of identifying detail on the old parish registers leads to speculation with earlier family events but later the sequence is that Collan Williams, 'sojourner of this parish' ,married Mary Rawlin on 24 December 1801 in Calstock and that their marriage was blessed with a son, named Collan. after his father and baptised on 16 December 1804. Again in Calstock on 7 October 1827, Collan Williams married Mary Elizabeth Gribbell and the couple saw daughters Elizabeth Gribble Williams baptised on 5 October 1828 and Mary Susanna Rawlins Williams baptised on 16 December 1831 as well as three sons, William in 1829, Henry in 1831 and Joseph in 1834.

As we have seen, mining in Cornwall was in decline and mining in parts of North America was just getting started. So it was that in 1857 the Jeffery family of Simon, Elizabeth and now three children, John Henry aged eight, Mary Elizabeth aged six and William Henry just two years old, together with Elizabeth's parents, Collan and Mary Elizabeth Williams, decided to exchange Cornwall for Keweenaw and made the long and arduous journey across the Atlantic Ocean, through the Great Lakes, along the Sault Canal, which with its opening just two years before in 1855 sidestepped the notorious St Mary's Rapids at Sault Sainte Marie, finally landing on the shores of Lake Superior. The exact details and timing of this trip are unknown as no ship's passenger list with their names has survived. What is known is that the final leg was aboard the 260ft wooden-hulled steamer *North Star* which was built in 1854 in Cleveland, Ohio. The vessel was under the command of Captain Ben Sweet and their initial landfall on the Keweenaw Peninsula was at Penn Mine, about five miles north east of Eagle Harbour on the western side of the peninsula. Eagle Harbour is a large natural harbour, so named as its shape resembles an eagle with outstretched wings, the head and neck of the eagle being the narrow entrance to the harbour. Despite its small size, with a resident population of only a few hundred, Eagle Harbour was the scene of much activity from the early 1840s and was a major stopping-off point for lake steamers carrying copper ore and shipping passengers and supplies to nearby mining communities. Its small population of less than 300 residents could boast two churches, six stores and three hotels by the early 1860s. By this time, Keweenaw mines accounted for up to 75 per cent of the copper being mined in the United States. The dense forests of the area and travel almost exclusively by boat must have been the first very noticeable differences for the Jeffery and Williams families. Cornwall has very little natural woodland. Additionally the climate here is very mild and whilst the summers in the Keweenaw are warm, winters are harsh with an average snowfall of around 20ft. Even the adjacent Lake Superior freezes in winter.

So it was into this new land, many thousands of miles from their native Cornwall, that the Jeffery and Williams families settled along with many other Cornish families and began working here, helping to build and sustain this new community and its new-found mineral wealth. Households in the community often included lodgers as there was a high transient population, using Eagle Harbour as a stopping off or staging point rather than a final destination. The 1860 US census, for example, shows Cullen Williams as aged fifty-six working as a labourer with his wife, shown as Elizabeth, forty-eight, with an eighteen-year-old servant girl, three clerks and an eight-year-old girl Lizzie Jeffery.

Lizzie was their grandchild, the second child of Simon and Elizabeth, born in Liskeard in 1850. As with any census record this is just a snapshot of who was living where on one particular day in that year. Lizzie, or Mary Elizabeth as she appears in the 1851 census in Cornwall, was probably staying temporarily with her grandparents at the time of the census. What is also a little confusing is that Collan's wife, who we have also met previously as Mary Elizabeth, is now shown simply as Elizabeth. Subsequent census and other records also record her as Elizabeth so there is a possibility that Mary Elizabeth died and that Collan remarried another Elizabeth but there is no documentary evidence currently available to support this. It is probably a case that she was known in the family simply as Elizabeth and that this is how her name is recorded on these documents.

The following census of 1870 shows that Colon, as his name is now given, together with his wife Elizabeth have moved a few miles north to Grant Township near Penn Mine, their original stopping-off point. This census shows that they were keeping a boarding house in the town and, unlike any census data here in UK, interestingly also values their personal estate as an estimated $2,000. This is equivalent to at least $50,000 by today's values or around £25,000. It seems that Collan and Elizabeth's decision to journey with their daughter and family to America was paying dividends when back in Cornwall as a labourer he would probably be earning less than $2 or £1 per week. By 1880 the census sees them back in Eagle Harbour and lists them as keepers of the Keweenaw County Poor House. Research indicates that they probably took over this position from James and Bathsheba Cocking, another Cornish couple, originally from Illogan near Redruth, who had kept the poor house for several years before them. It was not a large establishment; the 1880 census for example shows that it had just six residents, who had fallen upon hard times for a variety of reasons.

One other interesting household member in 1880 is Ida Williams, shown as aged ten and as being a daughter of Collan and Elizabeth. Given that the couple are now shown as seventy-seven and sixty-seven years respectively, this is probably either an enumerator's error or a child they had adopted, possibly after some tragedy had struck her family.

Collan Williams died on 16 December 1880 at a given age of seventy-seven years. The cause of his death is shown as cerebral apoplexy. He is buried in Pinegrove Cemetery, which is situated at the end of Pine Street, just outside Eagle Harbour. The names on the headstones and burial records of this cemetery read just like scores here in Cornwall: Berryman, Bowden, Mitchell, Nankervis, Polkinhorn, Pope, Richards, Rowe, Rule and Trebilcock are all to be found here, further evidence of the Cornish influence on this part of North America.

Collan's widow continued to live at Eagle Harbour. The last available record for her is the 1884 Michigan State Census where she is listed as living with a sixteen-year-old adopted daughter, Edith Cogan. No death record has been found for Elizabeth and as the full 1890 American census was destroyed by fire and she does not appear on the 1894 census of Michigan, it can only be said that her death probably occurred in Keweenaw somewhere between 1884 and 1894. Her name is not recorded as buried alongside her husband at Pinegrove.

The passing of Collan Williams and his wife Mary Elizabeth ended a chapter which had begun in east Cornwall and ended some 5,000 miles to the west. For their daughter, Elizabeth, married to Simon Jeffery, the family story was still unfolding. They had arrived in Keweenaw in 1857 with three children, John Henry, Mary Elizabeth and William Henry, all born in Cornwall. By the time of the 1860 census Simon, now shown as thirty-five and Elizabeth, thirty-four, had two more children, Cullen, who was born soon after their arrival in America and who was named after his maternal grandfather, and Ellen, who was less than a year old on the 1860 census. Also in the household were eleven other people, ten of whom are listed as miners and one as a servant girl. Again it seems that their household was a boarding house with room to take in quite a few boarders who would all have added a little to the family income each week. Listed close by is a Gribble family from Cornwall, possibly related to Elizabeth's mother who was a Gribbell, as it was spelt at the time, before she married Collan Williams. Simon's occupation at this time was a miner and he is known to have worked at several mines in the area, including Copper Falls, Phoenix and Connecticut.

The family did not, however, remain in the Keweenaw area. In the late 1860s they moved to Oneota Township, west of Duluth which is situated on the very south-westernmost shores of Lake Superior, in the state of Minnesota. Oneota was named after a Native Indian culture which developed in this area many centuries before the coming of the European. Duluth itself is perhaps best known these days as the birth place of legendary singer and songwriter Bob Dylan but back in the 1860s it was making its reputation in other ways. The town is named after Daniel Greysolon Sier Du Lhut, a French soldier and explorer who is reputed to have been the first European to set foot ashore here in 1679. He negotiated peace treaties with the native Salteur and Sioux Indians on behalf of the French nation and subsequently established fortifications in various locations around the Great Lakes to defend French interests. What probably drew the Jeffery family here was the fact that by the late 1860s Duluth had been chosen by Jay Cooke, the wealthy Philadelphia speculator, as the eastern terminus for the Northern Pacific Railroad which would have made it the only port with direct access to both the Pacific and Atlantic Oceans via rail links westward and lakes and newly constructed canals and waterways eastward. It was said at the time to be the fastest growing city in America, outstripping even Chicago and New York with huge business potential and plenty of work for all comers. In the first ever edition of one local newspaper on 24 August 1869 there was an article on its expected future prosperity which included the following paragraph, 'Newcomers should comprehend that Duluth is at present a small place and hotel and boarding house accommodation is extremely limited. However, lumber is cheap and shanties can be built. Everyone should bring blankets and be prepared to rough it.'

It was then to this fast growing township that the Jeffery family moved, initially to 'rough it' along with everyone else. But prosperity was to be very shortlived. Jay Cooke's empire came tumbling down in the stock market collapse of 1873 and development and investment in Duluth and surrounding areas ceased overnight. The community which had been thriving in 1869 almost ceased to exist within four short years. But Simon and Elizabeth Jeffery and their family stayed on. Perhaps they saw something in this area which many others did not. From the biographies of their children which we shall look at a little later, it would certainly seem that they made the right decision. The family are noted in the 1870 census as having nine children, John Henry, Mary Elizabeth, William, Colin and Ellen who we have met before plus Simon, eight, Emily, six, Henrietta, four and Susan two. All the children after William are given as born in Michigan. Simon's occupation is given as station engineer. Exactly what this means is not clear. John Henry is working as a miner and William as a labourer.

Despite the low points of the early 1870s the town's fortunes were on the up again within a few years and it was timber and mining which provided this welcome boost. Simon moved into public service, which like many local councils here in Cornwall was a part-time post additional to his normal work. He was elected as a town supervisor in 1871 and in 1875 became chairman of the Oneota Township Supervisors. In 1876 he was selected to serve as a juror at the local court quarterly sessions and in the same year was a local delegate to the district legislative convention. He progressed from this to become a Justice of the Peace in 1887. As well as holding this succession of public offices, the local press reports in May 1879 that he and his son Colin have established a dairy farm at a place known as Weller Farm and recommends that, 'townsfolk contact Mr Jeffery if they are interested in good home made butter.' Simon Jeffery died on 11 August 1888 at the age of sixty-four from 'inflammation of the bowels.' His death notice gives his occupation as dairyman. His widow, Elizabeth, lived on until 1902, living with daughter Emily and later her son Simon. Her death on 6 September 1902 at the age of seventy-three gives simply old age as the cause of death.

By this time their family were all grown and were engaged in a variety of occupations. With the help of census records, trade directories, local newspapers and other sources, it has been possible to follow this first generation of Cornish/American citizens and to see how they settled into a life which was for some of them, very different from anything their parents and previous generations had known in Cornwall. It is a story not of mining but is mainly centred around the lumber industry and the development of their lives runs parallel to the development of the community of Duluth and the surrounding area. The story runs from a time when it was necessary to 'rough it' to a time when the Jeffery family and many other pioneers of this area are seen to build a thriving community through their determination and hard work.

John Henry, the eldest son, born in Cornwall in 1849, had moved with his parents to Duluth around 1869. He was destined to become the best known of this generation of the Jeffery family. Initially he worked as a gang boss with the Lake Superior and Mississippi Railroad but later had a job carrying stone on a barge for a breakwater at the Superior, Wisconsin entrance to St Louis Bay on which Duluth is situated. He worked for three seasons at this job as an engineer aboard the tug *Amethyst*. During the 1870s he also obtained his Marine Engineers Licence and served as engineer or captain on two other tugs, firstly the *Fred and Will* and later the *Nellie Cotton*. This work mainly involved logging but there is evidence of other contracts with which the soon to be Jeffery Brothers Tugging Co. became involved, not least of which was the shipment of iron ore. The area was still a mining area, and shipping ore and processed iron to its final destination all formed a necessary part of the growing economy of the area, using the Great Lakes as vast highways even after the coming of a reasonably satisfactory road and rail system.

Logging was of great importance to the area. Timber was available from the surrounding natural forest in seemingly inexhaustible quantities and was the main building material used for new housing and other constructions necessary for the ever growing needs of the developing town and its increasing population. It was also shipped from many places like Duluth across the vastness of the Great Lakes waterways system to emerging and rapidly growing towns and cities like Chicago and timber from further east came in vast quantities across the Atlantic to Europe. The trees were cut in the forest mainly in winter as it was easier to drag them across frozen ground than across ground which had thawed in the spring and summer. They were roughly trimmed and prepared on site and then left near the banks of any number of convenient rivers to be floated downstream with the spring thaw. The first steam-powered commercial sawmill in this area was set up at Oneota around 1855 and very soon, sawmills and other processing plants were springing up all over the shoreline, sited along the lower reaches of the rivers and the shores of the lakes as these were the most accessible locations. The timber was formed into huge rafts which were then towed by tug to the mills and other sites for processing. Payment was by results, delivered timber being measured by the 'cord', a cord being equivalent to 16 cu. ft of timber and its value at the time anything from 65 cents to $1 per cord.

It was John Henry Jeffery's job to see that his rafted timber arrived safely at its destination, a task he successfully completed for several seasons without incurring any sort of accident or loss to cargo or crew. Exactly why the Jeffery family left their traditional mining activities and became involved in this completely different way of life is not clear, but John Henry was the first to make this change and at various times over the next forty years or so several members of the family in his generation and the next had an involvement in the timber business. Records of this involvement are not entirely clear for some family members but suffice to say that the family made, as we shall learn, a successful transition from miners to tug men.

On 6 April 1873, Captain John Henry Jeffery, as he was by then, married Miss Emma Demis Walker, second of eight children of Justice and Sybil Walker. Justice Walker was a carpenter by trade and his family had moved to Duluth not long before this marriage as census records from 1870 show them in Gardner, Grundy County, Illinois. Other records show that the family moved around quite a lot and at various times were resident in Ashtabula County, Ohio and also in McKean Township, Erie County, Pennsylvania. Again, as with most families of this era, the only probable reason for moving around was for purposes of finding employment, or better employment prospects in the fast developing America of the mid-nineteenth century.

In this same month April 1873, John Henry was given the job of engineer on the tug *Amethyst*. By the time of the 1875 Minnesota State Census he and Emma had an infant son, William Henry. In January 1880 John Henry acquired two lots of land in West Duluth from Mr A.J. Whiteman, valued at $1,100.

The next records of the family come from this same year of 1880 when the US census shows them still in Duluth with the addition of two daughters, Minnie Lucy, born in 1876 and Marthe Ellen, also known as Mertie, born in 1879. John's occupation is listed on this census as a tug captain.

He was at this time captain of the *Nellie Cotton* and a couple of years later, in 1882, he and his younger brother Simon purchased the tug *Amethyst* on which John Henry had previously worked and they completely overhauled her. It would seem that the *Amethyst* was in need of a lot of work before she could be made seaworthy again. She had not been in service since she was involved in a dramatic incident on Lake Superior in December 1879 whilst towing another tug *Siskiwit* whose engines had failed. The tugs were caught in a terrible snowstorm and in blizzard conditions, the tow rope parted and the *Siskiwit* began taking in water in heavy seas. The *Amethyst* bravely went alongside and successfully took off the crew of the other vessel but was herself taking in water and her captain eventually grounded her at a place called Belmore Bay. One man was killed by falling wreckage as they abandoned ship, the rest spending a night in hastily constructed lean-to shelters before trekking some fifty-two hours through uncharted blizzard ravaged forest, eventually finding the sanctuary of a logger's hut where they were given shelter until they could safely return overland to Duluth.

Also in 1882 John Henry acquired a land grant of 80 acres from the US Government and had established his family in their long-term home of No. 323 Fourth Avenue, Duluth. Throughout 1881 and 1882, the local newspapers carried advertisements for the Eureka Meat Market, Jeffery Bros, Proprietors. It is not clear if John Henry had any direct dealings with this business; certainly his younger brother Cullen was, as we shall see, a partner in this business but which of the others, John Henry, William or Simon may have been with him to give the name Jeffery Bros., is not clear. Perhaps one or more of the others was a partner, providing some funds out of their tug business which became known as Jeffery Bros., Towing.

Orders for ice could also be left with Jeffery Bros. for delivery around the town by J.B. Raab, a man originally from Germany who is listed on Duluth records as an ice merchant. Much of this ice would have been used in the fishing industry to help preserve the fish during transportation to outlying towns and probably further afield by road and rail links which were, by this time, greatly improved from the time when the Jeffery family had first arrived in the area some twenty years previously.

A further child named John Henry after his father was born in 1884 and throughout the 1880s John Henry's name appears on a variety of land deals. Among these, in 1887 he transferred three lots of land for $2,100, in 1888 he was involved in another land deal when he foreclosed on a mortgage to the value of $594 and in 1889 he purchased two more parcels of land in West Duluth for the sum of $1,000.

The family's decision to stay here when hard times hit in the early 1870s was now paying excellent dividends and Captain John Henry Jeffery was doing quite well financially from his timber towing business and expanding his interests with land and other dealings. In 1890 he became a founder member of the Zenith Branch (160) of the Independent Order of Oddfellows and two years later in 1892 he became Master of the tug *J.W. Bennett* which he sailed for six seasons, towing logs from various rivers around the western shores of Lake Superior to the sawmills and processing plants of Duluth. His eldest son, William Henry, became wheelsman on the *J.W. Bennett* working with his father from quite a young age. Also in 1892 it is reported that a new boiler was being installed into another Jeffery tug, the *John McKay*, allowing for increased steam pressure and consequently increased power.

Like his father before him, John Henry Jeffery also became involved in civic affairs in Duluth. The assassination of President McKinley in Buffalo, New York on 6 September 1901 saw a flurry of local activity to commemorate the man who was in his second four-year term as president and who has been said to be the most popular president since Abraham Lincoln, himself of course famously assassinated by a gunman's bullet.

Memorials and monuments were planned all over the country and John Henry Jeffery found himself appointed to the organising committee for the ceremonies marking the unveiling of the nation's first monument to McKinley in Duluth.

Despite his dabbling in other ventures, his main livelihood continued to be his work as a tug owner and captain and it was this which got him regularly into the headlines of the local newspapers, incidents such as in March 1904 when a reported 40in of ice was to be found in Duluth harbour and across a large stretch of the western end of Lake Superior, delaying the start of the logging season.

Another incident soon afterwards when workmen were busily engaged in trying to cut the tugs free from the grip of the ice to ease pressure on their hulls and again in 1908 when the tug bearing his name, *John H. Jeffery* tried unsuccessfully to make an early break free of her winter moorings by trying to smash the ice at Grignon's Yard where she was moored. The attempt drew quite a crowd but was unsuccessful as the ice was still too thick to break and the *John H. Jeffery* would have to wait a few more weeks before nature released the tug from her icy grip, ready for a summer season of intense activity. A far cry from the mildness of the winters here in Cornwall where snow and ice are a rarity.

Better news in that same year of 1908 was the marriage of his son John Henry junior and a party thrown by the family before the newlyweds departed for their new home in Winton, about 100 miles north of Duluth.

By this time the telephone had come to Duluth and Jeffery Bros. General Towing Line could be reached on Zenith 159.

But as with any life story, there must be some events which recall the bad times as well as those which record the good. One such incident was a court case where the Jeffery brothers' towing company was sued by a Mr Hurst for damages amounting to $2,000 for losing a vast quantity of logs from a boom whilst towing them from the Nemadji River to the sawmills. The first case fell down when the jury could not reach a verdict and a second trial was ordered with the plaintiff trying to prove negligence. A verdict was eventually returned against the Jeffery company and they were ordered to pay damages of $1,000, half of that sought by their accuser.

In November 1910 the local newspapers reported a dramatic fire on the Duluth waterfront which burned the tug *John H. Jeffery* almost to a total wreck. It appears that the boat had been working all day and the fire which provided the steam for her power had been banked up for the night. Somehow coal outside the firebox had ignited, and the blaze soon spread out of control. The 42ft-long vessel, built in 1868 by Willard & Mercer of Ontonagon, was originally known as the *Agate*, later renamed *John McKay* and then *John H. Jeffery* when he took ownership. Her value at the time is given as $3,500 but she was insured for just $2,000. Along with the *Amethyst*, built by the same company in 1869 and also owned by the Jeffery family company, she was one of the two oldest tugs still operating in the waters around Duluth. She was later rebuilt and operated for several seasons but another incident in October 1918 left her a complete wreck. This time a forest fire reached the lake shore and swept along the Duluth waterfront and completely destroyed the vessel on her moorings at Grassy Point. The 1910 and 1918 fires also destroyed the company's tool shed and parts of their office accommodation.

Further deep sadness fell upon the family on 14 November 1917 when John Henry's wife Emma to whom he had been married for forty-four years, died of heart failure.

All these events seem to have taken their toll on John Henry Jeffery for the prominent headline of the 18 August 1921 edition of the local newspaper reads, 'Capt. Jeffery, Veteran Great Lakes

Sailor, Duluth resident since 1862, Takes Life.' At the age of seventy-two, John Henry Jeffery, born in Callington in 1849 the first-born son of Cornish migrants Simon Jeffery and his wife Elizabeth Gribble Williams took his own life by hanging himself at the family home. According to the county coroner, Captain Jeffery was 'slightly demented' and grief over the loss of his wife four years earlier was said to be the probable cause of his 'deranged mind.'

A rather sad end to a life which had seen so much. From an early childhood in Cornwall through his growing up in his newly adopted country of America where he set up and ran a very successful timber towing business and dabbled in other business ventures, John Henry Jeffery appears to have made quite an impression, but obviously the loss of his wife and perhaps also the loss of one of his beloved tugs played on his mind to the extent where this life was tragically cut short.

He left an estate valued at $23,490, today that would be equivalent to the purchasing power of over $260,000, a sum shared between his four children.

Simon and Elizabeth's second child and eldest daughter, Mary Elizabeth, who was born in Liskeard in August 1850, is first found in Michigan records living with her grandparents, Cullen and Elizabeth Williams at the time of the 1860 census. Little is known about her early years. By the age of about twenty-two she was married to a man by the name of Martin Brown. Again little is known about him except that he was born in Pennsylvania in 1849, the son of Revd Lorenzo D. Brown, a Methodist preacher, and that he was a veteran of the American Civil War. His occupation on census and other records is teamster and carpenter.

Their family grew to include as many as eight children, Marietta, Martin, Susan, Minnie, Emily, Ellen, Cullen, Fannie and Franklin. It has to be said though that on some records it could be that there are less than eight and that one or two of them were shown by two names, for example Minnie E. on one census is quite possibly one and the same as Emily and Fannie appears also not to be consistent in name and comparative age from one record to the next. Such is the nature of researching these old records that, as we have seen with Elizabeth or Mary Elizabeth (Gribbell), the wife of Cullen Williams, names and indeed ages are not necessarily totally consistent through a series of census or other records. It was a time when remembering age and birthdays did not have the importance or significance that we place on it today and often, even today, many folk are known by a forename which is not necessarily the first name which appears on their birth certificate. What is known is that the Martin family maintained a home on No. 6 Street, Duluth and that at quite a young age, Mary Elizabeth suffered a lengthy period of ill health. Evidence of this comes from a newspaper article in February 1905 when it was announced under the headline, 'Double Wedding kept secret' that two of her children, Cullen, then twenty-one and Fannie, then just nineteen, had married, Cullen on 4 September 1904 and Fannie a few weeks before him on 25 July 1904. Cullen Brown married Helen Goshaw about whom nothing further is currently known and Fannie Brown married Clifford Keen, the son of the late Freman Keen who had been killed two years before in an accident with a streetcar. The newspaper explained that they had wanted to keep their weddings a secret over fears of disturbing their mother who had been in ill health for some time and also, the bridegrooms wanted to 'await better positions' before making the announcements. The extent of the secrecy of these two marriages can not be accurately gauged but it is most likely that reading about it in the local newspaper was not the first that the families knew about the marriages. It is far more likely that because they were quite a prominent family in the area and because of Elizabeth's ill health, they wanted a quiet wedding which was probably enjoyed by just a small family gathering on each occasion with the press finally getting wind of the events some time later, leading to them setting to work weaving their tabloid magic on the story. We may never know.

Cullen Brown and his new bride moved to Calgary, Alberta soon after their marriage and nothing further is currently known about them. Fannie remained in Duluth and it seems that her marriage, secret or not, was certainly not happy. The 1910 US census shows her living with her parents with no mention of her husband and by the next census of 1920 she is shown as divorced and is using her maiden name of Brown.

Simon and Elizabeth Jeffery's second son, William Henry Jeffery, who was their last child to be born in Cornwall in 1855, married in the late 1870s and he and his wife, Mary, formerly Mary Lemagie, are listed on the 1880 census living in Oneota village on the outskirts of Duluth. This census shows him as twenty-five which is accurate but shows his wife as fourteen. Again this seems to be quite an obvious error on the part of the enumerator as subsequent records show her as six years younger than her husband and to have been born in 1861. Mary was the daughter of a Belgian immigrant, Frederick Lemagie, who had come to this area as one of its earliest settlers in 1855. In William and Mary's household on this census record is a young girl, Susan Swanstrom, aged one year. Although Susan is listed as their daughter, she was in fact their niece, being the child of William's younger sister Ellen and Adolph Frederick Swanstrom. Ellen and Adolph were married on 15 August 1878 but Ellen had died on 3 June 1879, less than a week after Susan's birth. Young Susan is in fact noted twice on this 1880 census, once in the household of William and Mary and again in the household of William's parents. It seems that she was being cared for by close family members following the death of her mother and that both declared her to the enumerator, another example of how records can give rise to confusion and even doubt when researching family events.

But returning to William Henry, his occupation was in the timber industry at this time. He also had interests in road-building contracts and later dabbled for a while in real estate but his main occupation, as with his older brother, was working on the tugs on the lake, hauling logs.

His life was very nearly cut tragically short in 1882 when the local press reported on 'a sad case of insanity or temporary mental derangement.' We are told that William was under a lot of stress; he suffered from painful rheumatism and this, combined with the ill health of his wife, caused constant worry and anxiety which sometimes manifested itself in hallucinations. On this one particular occasion, he imagined that he was being chased by a group of men who, he said, wanted to hang him. He took refuge in the tug *Nellie Cotton*, where his brothers John and Simon found him. He cried out to them that this 'gang' were after him and promptly jumped into the harbour in an attempt to escape their clutches. Simon immediately jumped in after him and John threw them a line, which Simon grabbed, saving himself and his brother from potential drowning. William was taken to his father's house but ran away. He was eventually tracked down near the school in New London by his brother Cullen and another man, taken again to his father's house where he was confined for rest.

The incident does not seem to have had any lasting effect on his health as by the following year he is working as a tug captain, and he continued in this occupation until the end of the 1880s. He then had a short spell in real estate, followed by a spell as a street inspector, responsible for ensuring that the roads of the town were kept in good order and that repairs were carried out in a timely manner and to good standards. He was later to receive a promotion in this line of work as by 1896 he was inspector for a section of the main trunk road out of Duluth.

His return to the timber industry came shortly afterwards and he worked on the *John H. Jeffery* and *Cupid* in the next couple of seasons.

By 1899 he was working for the Stevens Towing Co. of Duluth and records tell us that this company was expecting to handle 100 million cu. ft of logs during the coming season. This is a huge amount of timber and this was but one of several companies operating in the area at this time.

His wife Mary was also involved in a variety of business transactions. Her name appears on several land sale deeds, including one to John Paden of the town of Superior where he was to prospect for iron ore and another for the sale of land to a Mr Brunt for $6,250, a sizeable sum equivalent in today's purchasing power to well over $150,000. Mary was also granted a licence in 1905 to sell and distribute milk within the Duluth town limits. William's health problems persisted as he is again reported to be suffering badly from rheumatism at this time. This did not, however, stop him from delving into local politics. He ran as a Democratic candidate in local elections in 1909. His main opponent was Lucian Merritt, the Pastor of Oneota Methodist Church and one of seven Merritt brothers who were part of a family who had made a fortune in iron ore in the Duluth area. The Merritt name features again a little later in our story.

William gave many speeches on a wide variety of topics in the run up to election day and fended off Merritt's claim that he was the better candidate as he had a college education and William did not. William countered that he would win by a landslide if all the college educated folk voted for Merritt and all the others voted for him. One hot topic for debate was the Duluth red-light district. The mayor was determined to instigate the council's resolution to do away with the red-light district but many businessmen felt that closing it down was 'not a good move'. It is not clear on which side of the fence William's loyalties lay on this subject.

What is clear is that when it finally came to voting day, the result was very close and William demanded a recount, a process which took over a month to resolve. The first count saw Merritt win by just four votes, 503 to 499. William then claimed that fifteen votes cast for him had not been counted, thus giving him a slender margin of victory and he demanded a recount. This managed to locate just one vote more for William but also found one vote for Merritt to be invalid, thus narrowing the gap between the two men even more to just two votes. William Jeffery's lawyers then came onto the scene with two more ballot papers casting votes for Merritt which they said were invalid, thus producing a tie in the voting. The matter was left for Judge Cant of the District Court to decide and after further counting and deliberation over the next couple of weeks, his ruling saw Merritt elected by the slender, but by then official margin of just six votes.

William Jeffery was not about to quit local politics. He ran again the following year but was again unsuccessful. He did however remain involved in community work. He served on the Merritt School Community Park Committee, a body charged with the improvement of local park and recreation amenities. It was the same Merritt family who had been the financiers of this project as had been his fierce opponents in the local election a couple of years previously. He also served on the committee of the Oneota and Hazelwood Improvement Club which was charged with supervising and maintaining the ice-skating rink at Merritt Park (that name again!), following a call from Mayor Prince that rather than rely on funding from the local authorities that students and civic organisations should provide free maintenance of the town's skating rinks during the winter season to save money.

William Jeffery died on 25 October 1914. Heart problems were ultimately the cause of his death. His obituary reported that he had been a Duluth resident for some forty-five years, that he had been manager of the Jeffery tug line since 1900 and that even before this he was deeply involved with tugs and the logging industry, even building his own tug the *Minnie Lamont*. He was survived by his wife, Mary and four children, Jessie, Susan, Ransom and Willis. He lies buried in Oneota Cemetery; the pallbearers at his funeral were fellow Lake Superior tug captains. His wife Mary died shortly after him on 25 August 1916.

The first child born to Simon and Elizabeth Jeffery after their arrival in America was Cullen, named after his maternal grandfather. He was born in Eagle Harbour, Michigan in 1857. Again. little is known about his early years until his marriage to Annie McDonald on 25 April 1882. Annie was born in Canada to Scottish parents. The ceremony was performed by Revd H. L. Shumate. Cullen was granted title to 160 acres of land by the US General Land Office in July of the same year. Unlike his brothers, Cullen did not go into the tugging business. He became a partner in a meat retail business. He and John Bradley were known as Jeffery & Co. and operated out of premises on Superior Street, Duluth. The company later became known as Jeffery & Doyle following a change of partner but lasted only a few years, closing in July 1890. Cullen and his family then moved to Fon de Lac, where the 1895 Minnesota census shows him as a farmer with his wife, Annie and three daughters, Edith, Mary and Elizabeth.

He and Annie soon had four daughters, Edith, Mary, Elizabeth and Christey, and the family continued to farm in St Louis County for many years. Cullen was also involved with road building and maintenance as a sideline to his farming business and records exist of a variety of payments to him for services rendered in repairing roads and as road foreman in the employ of the local council.

Annie passed away on 2 October 1916 in Solway Township but Cullen continued to work on and his farming interests continued. He became a director of the Munger Potato Growers Exchange when it was first formed in 1920, a post he retained until his death on 7 January 1923 at the age of sixty-five.

The second child born to the Jeffery family in America was Ellen in 1859. She married Adolph Frederick Swanstrom, the son of a Swedish immigrant family in August 1878. She gave birth to their first child, a daughter, Susan, in late May 1879 in Oneota but died less than a week later on 3 June of puerperal fever, a form of blood poisoning caused by infection contracted during childbirth. As we have noted previously, the baby was taken care of by members of the family after her mother's death.

Born in 1862 in Michigan and named after his father, Simon Jeffery was the youngest son of Simon and Elizabeth Jeffery. He, too, became involved in the tug business, working initially as an engineer for Joseph Lloyd in Duluth before becoming captain of the *John McKay*. He was married in December 1888 to Bessie Olive Call who was just seventeen years of age at the time of their marriage. She was the daughter of Ransom Call, a retired fisherman who became the Duluth courthouse janitor and his wife, Jane. Ransom Call was an American, born in Vermont and his wife, Jane, formerly Jane Teeple, was a Canadian citizen, her immediate family were from Ontario, but with an English background in previous generations.

In 1890, although still working in the tug business, Simon took possession of an initial grant of 126 acres of land through the US General Land Office and in 1893 he took on a further 160 acres. The 1895 Minnesota census tells us that by this time he and Bessie had a daughter, Mildred aged five. Also with them at this time is Bessie's widowed mother, Jane D. Call, and her unmarried sister, Ella.

August 1898 was a month when the family made the local newspapers for two very different reasons. The first was in connection with young Mildred's appearance in the Asbury Methodist Church performance of 'Red Riding Hood's Rescue', the second when Simon was arrested for destroying the beacon on Rice's Point at the entrance to Duluth harbour. Quite a contrast. Exactly why a man working with boats should destroy what must have been an important navigational aid is unclear as is his punishment for the misdemeanour.

The 1900 census sees the family living at Grand Avenue with Simon, his wife Bessie and three children, Mildred, ten, Ransom, three and Medora, one. Also in the household are his mother, Elizabeth, mother-in-law, Jane, sister-in-law Helen and a boarder. Another daughter, Helen, came along in 1907 and subsequent records confirm that Simon continued to be employed as a tug captain until illness in later life prevented him from working. He died at the young age of fifty-two years on 20 November 1913 following what is described as 'a prolonged illness'. He was survived by his wife, Bessie. No details are currently available on her life after the death of her husband.

Emily, the next child of Simon and Elizabeth, born in Michigan in 1863, married her late sister's widower, Adolph Frederick Swanstrom. Adolph was some twenty years older than Emily and she took very much of a back seat in their marriage as little is known about her. Research indicates that possibly their marriage was not the happiest, perhaps because of the age gap or the fact that they married hastily for the sake of late sister Ellen's child – we may never know. Census records for example suggest that Adolph and Emily did not live together all their married life. At least two such records show them at different addresses in the same town, so it seems that perhaps their relationship was not always stable. Adolph was quite an important figure in the administration of Oneota Township and also a businessman in the town. He was elected treasurer of the town in 1886, a post he held for at least three successive years and possibly longer. He was town postmaster by 1888 and running a general store in conjunction with this business. He sold his general store in 1893 to Leonidas Merritt, a name we have come across before, and Dan McDonald, a brother to Cullen Jeffery's wife, Annie.

Adolph continued in public service, petitioning for a better road surface for the roads of Duluth and holding offices such as watchman in the courthouse, as a clerk with O. Dahlsten and Co. and also as a labourer and self-employed grocer. He later became clerk in the Registrar of Deeds office from 1908 to 1913. He died in August 1921 and his wife, Emily, died in October 1929. Another of his many and varied jobs had been as a toll collector on the Duluth-Superior Bridge.

This first interstate bridge link between the two sides of the St Louis River, linking the towns of Superior on the Wisconsin side and Duluth on the Minnesota side, was opened in 1897. Part of it swung open to allow shipping through. An incident occurred some years later in 1906 when a ship hit the swing section before it was fully open, causing a 200ft section of the bridge to fall into the river below. It took a week to clear the wreckage from the river sufficient for shipping to again use the channel and over two years to repair the bridge structure. It was during this rebuilding that the company of Jeffery Bros began to advertise a ferry service for foot passengers, teams of horses and their wagons between Duluth and Superior. This was another excellent business idea on the part of the family even if it was to be just a temporary measure. The ferry operated only during the spell of two years or so whilst repairs to the bridge were being carried out but for two communities who had come to rely on a bridge to join them together, it would have been a vital link and a profitable one for the Jeffery family. The alternative was a 50-mile detour to the next bridging point upriver.

As can be seen from these biographies of this first generation of settlers to this area, the small settlement of Duluth and the surrounding area had been transformed in less than a generation from a small outpost where residents had to 'rough it' into a thriving town with industry and commerce developing all the time. Road and rail links were being established, local councils were elected and it would have been almost unrecognisable from the day when the Jeffery family first came ashore here in 1869. Henrietta Jeffery was a small girl of just three years old when the family arrived and she, like many others, saw this development first hand. She married Benjamin Franklin Neff in 1885 in Duluth. Benjamin was a Canadian with parents of German origin who, like most of the other residents of the area, had moved here seeking new challenges and opportunities. Benjamin became deeply involved in local politics and the affairs of the growing town. In 1888 he stood unsuccessfully for election to the village council, losing out to the candidate backed by the powerful West Duluth Land Co. who wielded a great deal of power and influence over land grants and development.

He was a carpenter by trade and had a successful business in partnership with John Morrison. Carpenters would have been amongst the busiest tradespeople in the community, building new houses for an ever increasing population and extending those already built. It is a bit of a mystery then why he should have given up that trade to become a grocer, which is his occupation on census and other records from about 1905. Perhaps it was forced upon him because of some sort of accident at work which made it difficult to continue in this trade, or perhaps it was his growing desire to enter local politics which led to the change – at present the answer is uncertain. What is certain though is that over the next ten years his involvement in community affairs developed to the stage where he stood for election as alderman in the town. The local newspapers carried, as they still do to this day, statements and articles championing their chosen candidate. One of these recommended Benjamin Neff to the electorate saying that he was 'a representative citizen who will faithfully study your interests' and one who was 'in favour of law enforcement.'

One of the main topics of debate at the time was, again, the reopening of the town's red-light district. We have noted discussion and debate on this subject before between William Jeffery and Lucian Merritt, and it was a topic which seems to have been to the fore at every election. The red-light district had been closed for a while but was recently reopened. It caused deep divisions in political circles in the town. Just before election time, the Revd M.S. Rice even took the matter into the pulpit and before giving his evening sermon, took the opportunity to endorse the re-election mayor R.D. Haven and recommend Benjamin Neff as alderman for the Fifth Ward. The reverend gentleman commended the mayor's determination not to reopen the red-light district and expressed the belief that Mr Neff was the kind of gentleman who would, if elected, uphold the mayor's stand. Despite this divine intervention Benjamin Neff lost the election by a majority of 159 votes to John Hogan, the Democratic candidate.

Life outside local politics continued and Benjamin and Henrietta's family also continued to grow. They had eight children, Gertrude, Luella, Olive, Samuel, Florence, Franklin, Elrose and William. As records of their children unfold we continue to see occupations which reflect the changing times from pioneer outpost to growing and thriving community. Luella became a teacher, Gertrude was a clerk, Olive went into sales and Elrose was a book keeper and comptometer operator with a hardware company – occupations far removed from their grandparents and generations before them who were true Cornish mining stock. Later records show that Franklin became a civil engineer and William, the baby of the family, became a truck driver.

Henrietta and Benjamin continued to live in St Louis County, Minnesota and although his ambitions in the greater political field seem to have been thwarted at an early stage, his interests in the local community and his grocery business continued, at least for the time being, to grow. His business was billed as being a 'Headquarters for Pure Food Goods' whilst outside of business his services to the community varied from juror at District Court level to chairman of the Duluth Boat Club, organising their carnival events.

Unfortunately his business hit hard times and the local newspapers of March 1914 published notice to creditors that the B.F. Neff Co. was filing for bankruptcy. It is not known what led to this dramatic change of fortune, neither is the outcome clear. Benjamin continued to operate as a grocer but on a much smaller scale after this date. He and his wife Henrietta lived on to see some of their children marry and bless them with grandchildren. Henrietta died on 24 March 1934 and Benjamin on 17 October 1940 in his eighty-first year.

The one remaining child of Simon and Elizabeth Jeffery was Susan, the baby of the family born in 1868. No firm knowledge of her has been obtained. It appears that either she may have died as a small child or died at the latest in 1895 as nothing positive can be traced of her through census or other records after this time.

So it was that this first generation grew with their new community. From relatively humble beginnings in east Cornwall they had moved on, made their mark and set down new roots. They had married into other families who had also come to this area from a variety of other parts of America and Europe for similar reasons, looking for work and new opportunities. Subsequent generations have continued to carry the family forward to the present day.

It is to one of these descendants, Steve Wilke, now resident in Thailand, that I am most deeply indebted for the major part of the research into the American side of this former Cornish mining family.

eleven

Lanyon, Pooley and Trewhella
Inherited Gifts

The parish of Ludgvan lies astride the busy A30, Cornwall's main road link into the rest of England. It is a very ancient place. Tonkin's history of Cornwall in 1739 tells us that its name is derived from Lug Van, meaning the hilly placed tower. This is appropriate as the church is on top of the hill. Tonkin also tells us that the place is mentioned in the Domesday Book of 1068 as being Luduham, and that it was one of the manors given by William the Conqueror to his half brother, Robert, Earl of Mortain. Before 1066 and all that, it was held by Alwin, and the population was said to consist of fourteen villagers and forty smallholders.

Dr Borlase, noted scholar and author of *The Natural History and Antiquities of Cornwall and Observations on the Scilly Islands* is buried here, having been rector of the parish for some fifty-two years. A later survey of Ludgvan around 1830 tells us that its population has risen from fourteen villagers and forty smallholders to a total of 1,839. Among these were Matthew Trewhella and his wife Julia and by the time of the first full census in 1841, they had helped to swell the population a little more with children, Julia, Matthew, Jane, Anne and William. Another daughter, Mary, came along soon after the census was taken.

Finding out exactly when Matthew was born has not been difficult as his death record from 1865 gives an exact age of sixty-one years, five months, twenty-one days, leading us back to a date of 8 October 1803 as a birth date. This of course assumes that he remembered his exact date of birth, which is possibly questionable for that era. As registration of birth did not come into effect until 1837, we have no means of being sure and we have to rely on baptism dates as the most accurate detail available to locate previous generations. Research has shown possibly two or three children of the name of Matthew Trewhella, or variations of the spelling, baptised around this area within a reasonable time span of October 1803. The 1841 census only gives Cornwall as a place of birth and is not specific to town or village and so we are left speculating. Suffice to say that the family name of Trewhella, in a variety of spelling interpretations, has been in this area for many generations before Matthew's time. It is a name you might have come across before, but our Matthew Trewhella was not the one who was lured into the sea by the legendary Mermaid of Zennor. The Matthew we are following is listed on the 1841 census as a miner. He had married Julia or Juliana Lanyon in Ludgvan Church in 1827. Juliana was the daughter of William and Mary Lanyon and she was baptised in Ludgvan on 27 January 1805. As with the name of Trewhella, the name of Lanyon is one which can be found in the parish registers of the area at least as far back as the early seventeenth century. Two families then, each having roots in West Cornwall for several centuries but now about to find themselves changing all of this for a new life many thousands of miles away on the other side of the Atlantic Ocean.

In 1813 in Cheshire, Connecticut, mineral deposits had been discovered on land occupied by a slave descendant known only by the name of Jinny. She had noticed some shiny rocks on a hillside on her property and examination by the eminent Professor Silliman of Yale University revealed that the rock was Barium Sulphate, a mineral much in demand in New York and other places in the manufacture of glass and paint.

Mary Trewhella was born in Cornwall in 1841 and married James Pooley in America. This photograph was taken on her wedding day in 1860.

Above: Edward James Pooley with his wife, Ida Irene (formerly Golden) and their two eldest children, James Eugene (Gus) Pooley and Edward Golden Pooley.

Opposite: The Pooley family at home in Meriden. Back row, left to right: Edward Golden Pooley, James Eugene (Gus) Pooley, Irene Golden Pooley. Middle row: Suzanne Pooley, Sarah Glock, Ada Glock. Front row: Alison Pooley, Catherine Wheeler Pooley. (My grateful thanks to Jennifer Fleisher of Montclair, New Jersey, great-great granddaughter of the original Pooley family for supplying their photographs and for permission to reproduce them here)

In 1838 financiers from New Haven organised a mining operation on the nearby Amos Bristol farm, close to the Fremington Canal, along which the mineral was barged to New Haven and from there by ship to New York. A second but shortlived mining operation known as Captain Peck Mines was also established a little further north. Rumours of a new mineral bonanza in America were soon spreading across to Cornwall where the centuries-old mining industry was in decline. One of the first to take advantage of this new opportunity was James Lanyon, who became manager of the Jinny Hill Mines in 1838. The exact date of his arrival in America is not known. He married in Cheshire, Connecticut to Lucretia Ann Brooks, a descendant of one of the founding families of the township of Cheshire. The couple came to own significant parcels of land on Bunnell Lane in the centre of the town and later owned the Lanyon Homestead on Main Street, where to this day there is still a reminder of the family in the street name of Lanyon Drive.

James managed the mine complex from 1838-1878 during which time the value of production peaked at around 4½ million dollars in a single year. Approximately 60-70 tons of ore were extracted daily from shafts which descended to 600ft below ground from which over four miles of passages and tunnels stretched out in all directions. When the Jinny Hills site became exhausted of its mineral wealth, the company bought the Captain Peck site and James Lanyon managed the whole site along with his brothers, Joseph and Henry.

James maintained close contact with his Cornish roots and family ties in his home parish of Ludgvan. One such family was that of his sister and brother-in-law, Juliana and Matthew Trewhella. Juliana and Matthew were the great-great-grandparents of Jennifer Fleisher of Montclair, New Jersey and it is to her that I am deeply indebted for this family story. She has carried out considerable research on the original emigrant families and on succeeding generations and what follows is the result of that research.

Matthew and Juliana travelled with their six children from Cornwall in 1845 and by 1850 they were able to purchase a tract of land adjoining James and Lucretia's property on Bunnell Lane. With these events, Cheshire witnesses the beginnings of a small Cornish stronghold only a few paces down an unpaved road from both the Methodist and Episcopal churches and the preparatory school, known today as the Cheshire Academy. The Lanyon and Trewhella homesteads sustained their families, heirs and close relations for approximately sixty-five years. In 1858 the Lanyon and Trewhella families were joined by a third Ludgvan mining family. John Pooley and his twenty-year-old son James travelled to America on the *New York* to seek work in James Lanyon's mine. In November 1860, James Pooley married Mary Trewhella, Matthew and Juliana's daughter who was born in Cornwall in 1841. While James Lanyon was a practicing Methodist, the Trewhella family seem to have followed Episcopalian traditions in America whose roots lie in the Anglican tradition.

Six years after their marriage, James and Mary Pooley were able to participate in the purchase of three adjoining lots on Bunnell Lane from Matthew Trewhella. This purchase was made in conjunction with Mary's older brother, William, her younger sister, Ann, their respective spouses and a fourth family by the name of Stevens who had come east from another Cornish-American stronghold in Ridgway, Wisconsin.

Meanwhile, Matthew and Juliana's oldest son, also Matthew, established a company called Trewhella Brothers Meat Market at the rear of the Bunnell Lane properties. Unfortunately no records of this business have so far been located to suggest how long it lasted or how well it sustained the family. We do know that life in mid-nineteenth century Connecticut was difficult. Cheshire town records show a high mortality rate amongst the first generation of Cornish-American descendants. James and Mary lost two of their eight children but Mary's brother Matthew was even less fortunate. All of his seven children born of his first wife, Margaret, died within the first few years of their lives. To make matters worse, Margaret herself died giving birth to the seventh child. In the same year Matthew remarried, taking a woman by the name of Victoria as his bride. Nothing further is known about her but of the four children she bore with Matthew three are listed in the death records in Cheshire Town Hall, all within the first few months of their infant lives.

Given such a tragic succession of events, one is curious to know what became of Matthew's eleventh and apparently only surviving child, Lillian Victoria, but no record has been found to indicate her fate. How traumatic it must have been to bury so many children and at the same time watch other families grow and thrive.

James and Mary Pooley's eldest son, Edward James, became a pivotal figure in transforming the lineage from skilled Cornish working class to American middle class. Although he is listed as a miner on early records, he had the good fortune to attend high school at the Episcopal Academy, also known as The Cheshire Academy, from 1872 to 1879. Although the school began as a college preparatory institution, during Edward James's time it functioned in a paramilitary capacity. Edward James's school records indicate that he was a corporal in Company B as well as a fraternity brother and a member of the sparring club.

The census record of 1880 lists Edward's younger brother John in the employ of a button shop in Cheshire at the age of thirteen. There is little doubt that this employer was anyone other than the Cheshire Manufacturing Co. in West Cheshire, an operation which was in reality a button factory, fashioning everything from dress buttons to military buttons and political campaign buttons. The company still exists to this day as the Ball & Socket Manufacturing Co., one of Cheshire's oldest manufacturing plants, having been originally established in 1845.

Tragically it seems that John became the third child James and Mary lost. He was just twenty-three years old when he died. His grave lies next to theirs in the Walnut Grove Cemetery in Meriden,

Connecticut. This small industrial town north of Cheshire became the new location for the Pooley family after the barite mines closed in 1878 following the lifting of tariffs on imported barite.

In 1879, Edward James Pooley entered Trinity College, Hartford, Connecticut. Founded in 1823, this is the second oldest college in Connecticut, Yale being the only one previously founded. Although he was only able to attend for a year, presumably because of cost factors, Edward gained the advantage he needed to work his way into a management level position with Manning Bowman, a company in Meriden who produced small household consumer goods like toasters, irons, coffee percolators and the like. Today, Manning Bowman items are classics of their time and some of their older kitchenware items are much sought after by collectors.

Whilst working at Manning Bowman, Edward Pooley met Ida Irene Golden, who worked there as a secretary. The couple married in 1899 and lived under the protective and domineering control of Ida's father, Eugene Golden, a Meriden patriarch of prominence and moderate wealth. He was a state senator, police commissioner and a supervisor at a metal works plant known as the Meriden Britannia Co. This was another of Meriden's manufacturing industries, founded in 1852 by Horace Cornwall Wilcox, son of wonderfully named parents, Elisha Bacon Wilcox and Hepzibah Cornwall. Wilcox's roots were in England but it is not known if the 'Cornwall' in his mother's name has any direct relevance to her birthplace or the ancestry of her family.

Meriden Britannia made Britannia Ware. Sometimes called 'grade A pewter', it is a mix of tin, copper and antimony, which is used for all kinds of household and decorative objects. It has also been called 'poor man's silver' as it was often used to make items which looked like genuine, and much more expensive silver. It was first manufactured in America as far back as about 1810 and first came to Meriden around this same time, manufactured by another man with a wonderful name, Ashbil Griswold. The availability of the necessary raw ingredients in the mineral mines of the area made Meriden something of a centre for the production of Britannia Ware and other household goods for several generations.

In 1898, Horace Wilcox's son, George, founded the International Silver Co. which, over a very short period of time, bought out many other manufacturing companies making Britannia Ware, silver plate and nickel products, establishing its headquarters in the former Britannia building in Meriden. Edward and Ida's second son, also named Edward, would come to work at International Silver as a photographer in later years, photographing their large selection of items for their sales catalogue and other advertising.

Although Edward and Ida's marriage was in many ways overshadowed by the forceful personality of her father, Eugene Golden, when their children came of age and earned excellent grades at high school there was no question that they would be without Eugene's blessing and sponsorship when they gained, as they all did, entry to college and further education.

Jennifer Fleisher tells us that Edward and Ida's first son, James Eugene, was her grandfather. He acquired the nickname of 'Gus' whilst studying as an undergraduate at Yale University, and he was the first known descendant of the Pooley, Trewhella dynasty to complete his education to PhD level. After Yale he went on to teach at the Sheffield Academy in Suffield, Connecticut before pursuing a graduate degree in classics back at Yale. Following his graduation in 1926, Gus taught at Williams College in Williamstown, Massachusetts and was then offered an assistant professorship in the Department of Classical Languages at the University of Vermont in 1928. Sadly his father Edward James Pooley died just a year before, unable to witness his son's great accomplishment.

During his working years, Gus's distinct intellectual interests dovetailed between his position at the university and his involvement with the Episcopal faith and the Cathedral Church of St Paul in Burlington. His scholarship in Latin segued into his study of the Bible, whilst his interest in medieval history created a natural bridge to Anglican Church history. He became popular in both for his informative and humorous speeches, which were always well attended. Simply put, he was a beloved community patriarch.

He served as registrar for the Episcopal Diocese of Vermont from 1954 to 1971; he was a vestryman of the cathedral and a delegate from the diocese to two Episcopal Church general conventions. In 1954 he was chosen as the Vermont lay delegate to the worldwide Anglican Congress.

Jennifer Fleisher also reflects upon the power of coincidence when examining the life of her grandfather, and says:

> He married Catherine Wheeler, a high school chum and through marriage acquired partial ownership of a one acre island purchased by Catherine's grandfather. Wheeler's Island is located off the coast of Connecticut near New Haven among a group of islands known as the Thimbles. Having visited Cornwall this summer, I can attest to the distinct similarity in 'feel' between Penwith, where the family originated, and this area of the Connecticut shoreline. I believe that Gus's life unknowingly became a reflection of his Cornish heritage, even though there is no indication from family lore that he was at all aware of the close connection to the sea that is at the core of his family's native culture. Gus and Catherine's first child, Suzanne, my mother, is also a mirror for that hidden family legacy. Having grown up on Wheeler's Island and able to participate in ownership of the property for most of her adult years, Suzanne has been steadfast in maintaining family traditions and our relationship with boats and the water. Suzanne was born on St Piran's Day, 5 March 1930.

Suzanne was born in Burlington, Vermont and experienced a proper upbringing as a professor's daughter. She enjoyed the benefits of her father's regular salary whilst the Depression was creating cruel hardships for many others. At the age of five she was joined by a sister, Alison, and the two girls grew up travelling frequently to Connecticut to visit relatives. They were able to spend time with their grandmother, Ida, known affectionately as Grandma Pooley and their Uncle Edward, Gus's younger brother when the family travelled to Meriden. Edward had assumed the duty and responsibility of looking after the Golden house and taking care of their mother after the death of Edward James. He worked as a professional photographer at International Silver following his college years spent at Lafayette College in Pennsylvania and Rensselaer Polytechnic Institute in New York. Ada, Gus's younger sister, attended Smith College and married a man of prominence in the banking world. They raised a family in the affluent suburb of New Canaan on the Connecticut coast. All of the Pooleys were involved to varying degrees in summer life on Wheeler's Island which was a focal point for meeting with the extended family.

Sadly though, this seemingly affluent and idyllic life was to have its tragedies. Alison developed leukaemia and died at the age of twelve. A few years later her mother, Catherine, suffered a mental breakdown, brought on by the combined trauma of her young daughter's death and the death of both her parents all within a four-year period. By 1947 Catherine was hospitalised with schizophrenia and never regained the personality she had prior to the breakdown. Gus and Suzanne were left alone to carry on their lives.

Fortunately their strong intellectual interests helped to sustain them and keep them going. Suzanne was able to attend the University of Vermont at little cost because of her father's teaching position. Upon her graduation she began graduate studies at Columbia University in New York City where she earned a Master's Degree in Speech and Theatre in 1952. In 1956 she began a teaching position at the State University of New York in New Palz where she met Siegel Fleisher, a colleague in the English department. They married in 1960. The year 1965 proved to be one characterised by sadness, joy and significant change. The sadness was the death of her mother and Uncle Edward, on a happier note she gave birth to a daughter, Jennifer, and also assumed partial ownership of Wheeler's Island.

Jennifer recalls her childhood as being enlivened by trips to her grandfather's house in Burlington. She recalls visiting him at the Shelburne Museum where he was a volunteer worker, giving guided tours to visitors. In later years he lost his independence when his eyesight began to fail. Jennifer recalls:

One of my favourite memories is of sneaking up to him as he sat in his big black leather armchair in the living room and running my hand over the stubble of his balding head. Gus would feign ignorance that I was there, all the while making giggling noises which would make me laugh. A gentle soul, he allowed me to play this prank again and again, each time pretending he had no idea what was giving him such a strange sensation.

In 1987, a visit to Burlington for Suzanne's fiftieth high school reunion took her and Jennifer to the University of Vermont Classics Department. To their surprise, some fifteen years after Gus had taught there, they found the chairman of the department treating them like royalty when they entered the room, sharing with the assembled company recollection after recollection of Gus's contributions to the department and of his humour – 'It was a moment of true pride in connection with my grandfather, which I cherish. He spurred so many to value the intellectual life and reminded us never to take ourselves too seriously in that pursuit.'

Jennifer also acknowledges her debt of gratitude to her mother for raising her in a family structured around a love of learning. Jennifer always nursed a compelling desire to pursue a career in the arts. Following ten years of classical fine art training in portraiture and landscape oil painting, she created and managed a mural company out of her own home for five years. Her most significant contributions include a portrait of Martin Luther King Jnr on a mural at the National Constitution Centre in Philadelphia, Pennsylvania and a completely original mural celebrating the diversity of the student body of the alma mater, Rutgers University, New Brunswick, New Jersey. Despite these successes in the art field, powerful influences from her childhood have also helped her to develop her writing talents. Currently working in an administrative 'day job' time is left to write in the evenings as well as continuing with her painting. As Jennifer notes in conclusion to her story:

Merely four generations ago my family's Cornish ancestors arrived on American shores with little more than the hope of a job in a mine. Like many Cornish families, resilience, hard work and good fortune have carried us to this point in time. May I have the presence of mind to realise the gifts I have inherited and to put my days to good use.

twelve

Richard Lawry
'Wild Dick'

About as far west as you can go in Cornwall you will find Lady Downs marked on the map. It lies between Zennor and Nancledra. It is a place with evidence of some of Cornwall's earliest inhabitants. Chysauster, Castle an Dinas and Sperris Quoit are all marked here along with numerous other cairns, stone circles, ancient field systems and reminders of pre-Christian times. It is also a land of many legends. It is near here that the Mermaid of Zennor lured her lover to the deep and here, too, that Cherry of that same parish of Zennor, a poor girl who left home to seek work, fell for the charms of a kindly man who, as the legend tells, could be seen in his true form of a fairy gentleman only with the aid of his special eye drops. Cherry was banished from his service when he found out that she knew his secrets but it is said that she stills roams Lady Downs looking for her lost love and on nights when the moon is chased across the sky by the clouds, it is easy to see many lost souls traced in the rocky outcrops. It is also the place where, one dark night in 1865 the whole population were awoken by the mournful tolling of the church bell. Some thought the Devil himself was at his work, calling lost souls, but investigation confirmed that it was a cow, chewing quite contentedly on the bell rope in Morvah Church.

But our story is not of fairies and mermaids but of farmers and miners, for the reality of the nineteenth century in this part of Cornwall was of a harsh living forged out of the solid granite of these upland moors. It was hard work. Farming and mining were the main activities of most families and one such family were William and Amelia Lawry. The 1841 census tells us that William Lawry lived with his wife, Amelia and children Lydia, fifteen, Elizabeth, eleven, John, eight, Mary, six and Emily aged just one year at Ridgoe in Gulval parish. William was an agricultural labourer and the family had been in the area for many years. The family name of Lawry is one which can be found amongst the earliest parish registers of the area. Even a quick search of records will find the name of Lawry on a variety of documents through the eighteenth and nineteenth centuries. Not all of them are found to be good and honest citizens, for example Sibella Lawry, 1764, before the court to establish paternity of her child born 'out of wedlock'. Also, Jane Lawry, 1776, described in Quarter Sessions records as 'a rogue and vagabond'. One William Lawry was fined the sum of 40s in 1810 for failing to do his duty and act as a juror at the Quarter Sessions. This equates to at least £150 by today's purchasing power and was a vast sum to find in those days when agricultural and mining workers counted their daily wages in mere pennies. There were others, however, who seem to be of better character. A lease dated 1803 gives lands at Tregaminion in Morvah parish to William Lawry 'for 99 years or three lives', not something which would be granted to anyone of bad character. This type of lease guaranteed the land to three generations of the same family and was a way of the landlord ensuring that his lands were well looked after for a long period and also had benefits for the tenants in that they had a home for themselves and two subsequent generations, provided of course that the terms of the lease were met which generally would have meant paying the rent on time, keeping the property in good order and complying with any other conditions of the lease which often included things like 'harvest journeys', which meant working for at least a day or two a year at harvest time for the landlord.

Other Lawry entries in records of the time show that in 1825 William Lawry was a signatory at the swearing in of Morvah Churchwardens.

It is not clear if this is one and the same as the William from the 1841 census, as detail on some of these old records is a little sparse but one record certainly relating to our Lawry family is a baptism entry dated 12 August 1832 which shows John, son of William and Amelia of Ridga, as it is spelt here, with William's occupation as labourer.

John became a miner, working at one of the many mines hereabouts and by the time of the census in 1861 he is to be found with Honor, his wife and their children Mary, five, John, four, and Richard, aged one year living at No. 5 Lady Downs, Towednack. Lady Downs is but a dot on the map, said at one time to consist solely of two farms and an equal number of Methodist chapels. It is within the ancient Cornish Manor of Amyll and Trylle, which came into the family of the Davyes and Gilberts of Treilissick back in 1679 as part of a marriage settlement between William Davyes and Catherine, daughter of Humphry Noy.

By the following census in 1871 John Lawry's family had grown to six sons, John, Richard, William and Thomas, who were twins, James and Andrew and one daughter, Mary. The place of abode was now Mill Downs, Zennor. John the father was described as a 'tin miner and farmer of five acres.' A smallholding of just 5 acres in this part of Cornwall would not provide an income sufficient to sustain all the needs of a family of this size and so, like many others, John worked at one of the local mines and grew sufficient for his own family needs and perhaps a little extra to sell to supplement his income as a miner. His mining occupation was to lead to his premature death. He died of the dreaded 'miner's lung', a disease caused by years of inhaling dust in the mines which eventually clogged up the lungs to such an extent that breathing became difficult and finally caused a painful and often premature death. Sadly, two of his sons would also die of this terrible disease whilst working in mining in South Africa some years later.

One of John's sons, Richard Lawry, got himself something of a reputation for getting into mischief and although there is no record of him doing anything which got him into trouble with the law, he did earn himself the nickname of 'Wild Dick'. It was possibly his love of boxing which got him the nickname; by all accounts he was quite tall with a long reach, much suited to that particular sport.

In his teenage years Richard Lawry met a girl from the village of Lelant by the name of Elizabeth Ann Martin. She was a distant cousin through the Pengelly family line and was the daughter of Christopher and Elizabeth Martin. The 1871 census shows the Martin family living at Carbis, near Lelant. In addition to Elizabeth Ann there are four other daughters, Wilmot, Emma, Nanney and Kate and one son, Christopher, named after his father.

As we know all too well, this was a time when the economy of Cornwall was on a downward spiral and so it was that on 11 October 1879, Richard Lawry set sail with the Martin family on board the *Piako* out of Plymouth, bound for Lyttelton, New Zealand. Perhaps Elizabeth Ann was a factor in his decision to go to New Zealand, but his 'Wild Dick' reputation was certainly a concern to his family, who feared that one day he might get himself into real trouble and so encouraged him to leave and begin a new life elsewhere.

The *Piako* was a 1,075-ton vessel, 215ft long and 34ft wide, built in Glasgow and launched in December 1876. Her first voyage to New Zealand for her owners, the New Zealand Shipping Co., took her ninety-nine days. This was about an average time for the journey. Her second voyage, under Captain W. Boyd, began in Plymouth on 20 November 1877 and she arrived in Port Chalmers, near Dunedin on New Zealand's south island just seventy-six days, twelve hours later, almost breaking the record for the voyage. Her third voyage saw amongst her 317 passengers the Martin family and Wild Dick Lawry.

Also aboard the *Piako* on that voyage were several other Cornish families, among them Philip Oliver, a carpenter from Roche with his wife, two children and his younger brother, John; the Potter family of John and Emma with their four children from Camborne; Stephen Vosper, a seventeen-year-old wood turner, son of Thomas, a chairmaker and Eliza Vosper also from Camborne; Richard Osborne, bootmaker of Plainangwarry, Redruth; and James Lobb, mason from St Neot with his family. A mix of occupations, all with one thing in common – they were looking for a new life and better prospects on the other side of the world.

The voyage seems to have gone quite smoothly for the first four weeks or so, with the usual mix of weather to be expected in the Atlantic Ocean. Time on board these migrant vessels was passed in a variety of ways, deck games, lessons for some of the children and a lot of time simply gazing at the sea. Sometimes the mood was improved by the sighting of schools of dolphins jumping alongside the ship, whales too were quite a common sight in some latitudes and flying fish were often said to land on the decks. But there was in reality little for the passengers to do and nowhere for them to go on such a small vessel with so many passengers. Some passengers who could read and write kept a diary of their journey and many of these have survived down the years. They talk of many days when the weather was either too bad to venture on deck or so hot and windless that the sea was like glass. They sometimes tell of the death of a passenger, often a small child destined to be buried at sea, never to know their new homeland. But in the main, these diaries tell of long days with little to occupy the passengers.

The voyage of the *Piako* on this occasion, however, did have one, almost catastrophic incident. About 160 miles off Pernambuco on the coast of Brazil, smoke was seen coming from the forward hatch. In an attempt to see exactly what the problem was, the hatch was opened and the inlet of air caused a fireball with flames of 20ft in height gushing from the hold. Part of the cargo was ablaze. The hopelessly inadequate fire hose on board had no effect whatever in quenching the flames and an attempt to reach it from below was driven back by heat and smoke. The captain gave orders to make for Pernambuco and some passengers began to panic as the lifeboats were lowered. Just as he gave the traditional order of 'women and children first', a sail was sighted and this, and the captain's calming influence, possibly helped by the fact that he was wielding a pistol and appeared quite prepared to use it on anyone who decided to take the law into their own hands, soon had everyone on board listening to his orders and going about things in a much calmer manner. The sail belonged to the *Loch Doon*. She was one of a total of eight ships of the Loch Line, owned by Messrs D. & J. Sproat of Liverpool and chartered to take passengers and cargo on the run from England to New Zealand. It took her about three hours to steer a course close enough to the *Piako* to take on board her passengers. But this operation was not without its incidents. The transfer from one ship to the other was carried out by breeches buoy, apparatus adapted from an invention by another Cornishman, Henry Trengrouse, after he had witnessed the tragic events of HMS *Anson* at Loe Bar in 1807. When it came to Elizabeth Martin's turn, the ships drifted closer together with the motion of the waves, the line slackened and she fell into the sea. The quick actions of one of the crew who pulled the line tight possibly saved her from more than just a dip in the cold ocean. Apparently the only harm caused by the incident apart from a soaking was that is gave her a lifelong fear of open water. With most passengers safely on board the *Loch Doon* and with only the crew and a few passengers left on board *Piako* fighting the fire, both ships then made for Pernambuco. On arrival they found even more trouble as the port was quarantined following an outbreak of smallpox; 400 people a day were said to be dying from the disease. The captain decided to make for a small, uninhabited island, known as Coconut Island, about seven miles from Pernambuco.

Here he landed his passengers. He then scuttled his ship in shallow waters to extinguish the fire. She was raised again soon afterwards and there was found to be very little fire damage to her overall structure.

Most of the passengers' baggage and other cargo in the forward hold was destroyed, either by the fire or by the effects of scuttling the ship. Happily however, no lives were lost in the incident. Passengers and crew were marooned on Coconut Island for about nine weeks before repairs were completed. This in itself was quite an ordeal, the island was quite small, just a small grove of coconut trees surrounded by sand. Temporary shelters were erected using sails and other equipment from the ship, but it must have seemed like a classic desert island castaway situation for the passengers. Food and other supplies were brought in from the *Piako* until finally repairs were completed and the ship resumed her voyage to Lyttelton where she arrived on 5 March 1880, 145 days after leaving Plymouth.

The *Piako* continued to make the run from England to New Zealand with emigrants and was later sold to a German company as a cargo ship. She was lost without trace somewhere in the southern oceans in 1900 whilst transporting supplies from Melbourne to the troops fighting in the Boer War in South Africa.

Back in New Zealand, there must have been great relief when the ship finally reached her destination. Richard's elder brother John came to meet the ship. He had sailed to New Zealand some time before to seek a new life and was able to help Richard find a job. The new life began on a positive note, with plenty of work for Richard and the Martin family. To add to the happiness of their new life, on 11 June 1881 in the Register Office in Christchurch, Richard 'Wild Dick' Lawry married Elizabeth Ann Martin. Their first child, a son named Richard Henry, was born on 2 January 1882. Richard and Elizabeth are listed in local directories as hotel keepers in Sydenham, Christchurch at the time of the birth of their first son and other records also list his occupation as publican and boxer. It is thought that during his time in New Zealand he was often a sparring partner for the great Bob 'Ruby Robert' Fitzsimmons, the Cornish triple world boxing champion who had emigrated to New Zealand as a young man.

Three further children were born to the Lawry family in New Zealand, Christopher John, 6 December 1882, Arthur Ernest, 19 February 1884 and Wilmot Jane, 6 October 1886.

On 5 July 1889 the family left New Zealand, bound for England. Exactly why is not clear but it seems that the decision was quite a hurried one. There was some sort of incident involving Wild Dick which prompted a hasty decision to leave the country. Almost immediately after their arrival in Cornwall, Wild Dick was on board ship again, this time across the Atlantic to America. Four of his brothers, Andrew, Samuel, James and William, were already in Ishpeming, Michigan working in the mines there. They were all boarding in the household of their sister Mary and her husband, Dick Nichols. Wild Dick's wife, Elizabeth, together with their four children joined him in Ishpeming in 1890. It was here on 18 May 1893 that their fifth child, Mabel Deane Lawry, was born.

Ishpeming was a town built on the discovery of iron ore there. In 1846, a local Indian by the name of Madji Gesick led explorer Philo Everett to a place the local Indians called the Shining Mountain. It was, in fact, a huge mass of iron ore measuring some 180ft high and over 1,000ft wide. It was later named Jasper Knob and the area became known in mining circles as The Lake Superior Location. Early settlers named the new town they built on the site Ishpeming, which is taken from the local Chippewa language and means 'on the summit'.

It is an appropriate name as the city lies on the dividing ridge between Lake Michigan and Lake Superior. Today it is the home of the US National Ski and Snowboard Hall of Fame but in the nineteenth century, its fame came from its iron ore deposits and many of its original settlers were from Cornwall where the mines were closing and the economy sliding downhill just as fast as some modern-day skiers.

Along with their expert knowledge of mining, the Cornish took to their new homes their love of music. The playing of music and singing are as traditional to Cornwall as its tin and copper mining, and brass bands have been a part of the Cornish entertainment scene since at least the 1850s. It is believed that the Lawry brothers at one time played in the Towednack Band, whose first engagement was in 1852 at the opening of the West Cornwall Railway at Penzance Station. Richard Lawry, no longer it seems Wild Dick, later played cornet in the Ishpeming Band for several years. He also became an active member of the First Methodist Church and was a member of the choir there. He also played in the Sunday School orchestra of the Methodist Church. He was not the only family member to have the gift of music. His youngest child, Mabel Deane Lawry, became a prominent singer, performing all over America with the John Philip Sousa band. She married and became Mabel Chamberlain and it is to her son, Dick Chamberlain, (in full, Richard Henry after his grandfather) now resident in California, that I am indebted for this family story. He recalls that Mabel retained some of her Cornishness, especially in some of her endearments to young children like: 'The dear's of 'em' and 'God bless 'is baby 'eart.'

He remembers his grandparents Richard and Elizabeth and relates that, like any true Cornish marriage, Elizabeth's word was law. She was quite short, again I suppose typically Cornish, but as her husband was heard to say on many occasions: 'Ma 'd be some small but she'd be some fierce.' Elizabeth was a 'staunch no nonsense Methodist' who took the view that anything pleasurable was probably sinful as well. She became a Christian Scientist, accepting their belief that 'God is Love', which seemed to transform her into the gentler, kinder person that Dick remembers from his childhood. When once asked if he intended to join the Christian Science Church, Richard replied, 'Naw, naw, too much Mary Baker Eddy, not enough Jesus Christ.'

While Richard and his family and four brothers boarded with his sister Mary in Ishpeming for a time after their arrival, they all ate together and at meal times the men would soon engage in loud discussions on mining, local politics and anything else likely to bring about friendly disagreement and argument. It was at this stage that Mary, also a diminutive figure like her mother, would slam a pan on the iron stove and shout, 'Lawry, shut the mouth of 'e.' Silence would reign for a while but if the noise grew again to a crescendo, she was not averse to striking the nearest Lawry head with a pan from the stove, which again had the immediate effect of bringing relative peace and quiet to this somewhat overcrowded household.

When Mary, or Auntie Nichols as everyone called her, became ill in her later years, her brother Richard would often appear at the door of the house saying that he had come to spend some time with his sister. He would sit silently at the bedside of his ailing sister, holding her hand until it was time to catch the evening trolley bus back to Salisbury, the little mining community where he lived, about three miles from Ishpeming. He would put on his hat and leave without a word; the bond between them was very strong.

Richard and Elizabeth celebrated their sixtieth wedding anniversary in Ishpeming. At around this same time events were taking place celebrating the centenary of the town and among these was a pioneer's picnic. Prizes were awarded in a host of categories including 'the longest married couple on the lot.'

Having achieved their golden anniversary, Richard and Elizabeth easily won this contest and were rewarded with a prize. Glenys Jachimski, great-granddaughter of Richard and Elizabeth, tells me that she was a front-row witness to the events which followed. She says that the master of ceremonies made a big fuss over them having been married for so many years and about the wonderful prize they had won, a voucher for $3 to be spent at the local pharmacy for medications.

She remembers quite clearly the look of surprise on Elizabeth's face and the look of disgust on the face of Richard for here stood a man in his late seventies who had never even swallowed an aspirin and all they got for a prize was a certificate for medications, not cash which they could have put to good use. Elizabeth was called upon to receive the award and say a few words to the assembled crowd. For the first time in her life it seems she was lost for words.

She asked, 'Pa, Pa, what shall I say?'. In reply, Richard said in a rather disgusted sounding voice,

'Don't say nawthin'. Whether the crowd appreciated the feeling in his voice or whether they simply thought he was lost for words I am not sure but this shortest of acceptance speeches was broadcast over the loudspeaker system and brought much laughter and amusement to those assembled for the celebrations.

In his later years, when the weather permitted, Richard Lawry had taken to walking the six miles or so from his home to the local cemetery to visit the graves of those who had departed this life, including his son, Christopher John. After cleaning around the graves he would then walk back the six miles to home. The walk gradually became too much for him and one day he appeared at the door of his grandson, Gordon, Glenys Jachimski's father, who lived about a mile from the cemetery, and declared to Gordon's wife Dorothy that the walk had made him 'some tired and thirsty.' Dorothy was quite alarmed at his pale colour and general state and she immediately telephoned her husband at work to come and drive Richard home. This was done and their followed an edict from his daughter Wilmot Jane or Jen as she was known, with whom he and Elizabeth were living at the time, that he was no longer to make the walk. Richard, in true Cornish stubborn fashion, was having none of this and following some 'negotiation' it was finally agreed that Jen would telephone Dorothy when he left home. He could then make the walk, calling to 'check in' with Dorothy as he passed their house on his outward journey and calling there again on the way home to wait for a lift home when Gordon finished work. He never stopped making a fuss over this arrangement saying that he had walked all over the area on his own for many years and saw no reason to stop now, just because he was getting older. During these stopovers waiting for his lift home, Richard would recall many stories of his youth to his great-granddaughter Glenys who, although herself now approaching her eightieth year, tells me that it seems like just yesterday that she was in his presence.

Richard Henry Lawry died on 12 June 1942 in his eighty-second year and just a day after his sixty-first wedding anniversary. His dear wife lived on for little over a year after his passing and died on 2 September 1943.

Perhaps the regular engraver of the headstones in the cemetery was away at war when she died as the 'z' on her inscription is carved backwards.

My most grateful thanks to Richard Henry Chamberlain and to Glenys Lawry Jachimski, grandson and great-granddaughter of Richard 'Wild Dick' Lawry for details of their family story.

thirteen

Elizabeth Uren
St Keverne to Salt Lake City

The village of St Keverne lies on the eastern side of the Lizard peninsula, about ten miles from the town of Helston. The peninsula juts out into the English Channel and over the years has trapped scores of unfortunate vessels on its rocky shores, sometimes with huge loss of life. Perhaps the most notorious of the offshore reefs here are the Manacles, the scene of some of the worst shipwreck disasters in Cornish maritime history. Lying as they do less than a mile offshore, their jagged teeth are there waiting to snare any vessel which comes into contact, and have seen wrecks such as the *John* in 1855, an emigrant ship on passage from Plymouth to Quebec when over 300 lives were lost. The *Mohegan* and the *Bay of Panama* at nearby Nare Head also later fell victim to this rocky shoreline. Countless ships down the years have been lost here even up to modern times. But despite the dangers, the men of the area have for many centuries earned their living from the sea as fishermen and sailors. These occupations, together with farming, gave most families their daily bread back in the nineteenth century when our story of Elizabeth Uren begins to unfold. She was baptised on 14 September 1828 in the Parish Church of St Keverne, the daughter of Thomas and Mary. Her baptism record shows her father as a seaman, although some baptism records for her siblings show him as a labourer. Exactly when and where her parents married is unknown as a search through St Keverne and the adjacent parishes has failed to locate a marriage for them but the parish registers do vividly recall that tragedy followed them throughout their short marriage. A daughter, Betsy, was baptised on 2 July 1827 but died as a small child and was buried on 22 May 1828. A son, Thomas, was baptised on 25 April 1830 and buried just two months later on 30 June. It was quite a common practice at this time to give a subsequent child the same name as a deceased sibling and so we find another son, also named Thomas, baptised on 24 July 1831. He, too, sadly died as an infant and was buried on 16 October that same year at the age of just four months. Thomas the father also died young. He was buried on 14 August 1836 at the age of just forty-two years, leaving Mary a widow with their three surviving young children, Elizabeth, John and Betsy. The census of 1841 shows the family living at Churchtown, St Keverne with Mary employed as an agricultural labourer. Elizabeth is not in the household, she is out at work living in as a servant girl with Mr William Williams and his family at Roscrowgie, a farm just a couple of miles west of the village of St Keverne, close to the modern-day Goonhilly Satellite Earth Station.

Meanwhile, just across the Helford River in the parish of Constantine the 1841 census shows us a farming family of Emanuel Ould, with a given age of fifty years with his wife, Jane and children Emanuel, fifteen, Jane, fifteen, John, ten and Mary, nine living at Bar House, Helford Passage. The 1841 census is, as we have noted before, notoriously inaccurate with age and the fact that Emanuel and Jane are both shown as being fifteen does not necessarily indicate that they were twins. Emanuel was probably seventeen at the time of the census, having been baptised in Constantine on 23 November 1823. Other members of the extended Ould family, as well as being farmers, were also ferrymen, taking passengers across the Helford River.

A ferry service has operated here since the Middle Ages and still runs today, although on a slightly different route from the time of the Ould family. The property they occupied at Bar is shown on the 1841 tithe map as a small farm at the junction of the Helford River and Port Navas creek. It is listed on census records next to Budock Vean. Now a top country hotel with its own golf course, Budock Vean was then the family home of Francis Pender, listed as an attorney on the 1841 census. His father had been a packet agent in the heyday of the Falmouth Packet shipping service and Francis had been an alderman and mayor of Falmouth in earlier years. He was joined in his law firm by James Genn whose family were originally from Virginia in America, to form Pender & Genn, later to become Genn & Nalder and then Nalder & Son, a law firm still to be found here in Cornwall today. As far as can be seen from current research, the farm at Bar, Helford was owned at the time by the Pender family and tenanted by the Ould family who were there for several generations from around 1720 to the end of the nineteenth century. Nothing is left now of the farm house except for a ruined wall with an old fireplace, situated in the grounds of a more modern property. Members of the Ould family remained in and around the Mawnan and Constantine area even after they left Bar Farm and their descendants still live locally to this day.

It is interesting to note that current research also indicates that the name of Emanuel or Emmanuel has occurred in each Ould generation from at least the late 1600s and that John, shown as aged ten on the 1841 census and who later farmed at Bar, also gave this name to one of his sons. This Emmanuel Ould moved the short distance from Helford to Falmouth where he became a coachman at Arwenack House, the home for many generations of the Killigrew family. Another Ould family member later continued the trend of working with horses and became head groom at Buckingham Palace.

But to return to Elizabeth Uren. She met Emanuel Ould of Constantine and the couple were married in Mawnan Church on 16 May 1850. The marriage certificate shows both of them as 'of full age', his father as Emanuel Ould, labourer and her father as Thomas Uren, labourer. It also shows his occupation as 'servant'; exactly where he worked and what his duties were, we are not told but it was probably in one of the large houses in the area, possibly Budock Vean, which we have mentioned before or nearby Trebah, or Glendugran.

Very shortly after their marriage Emanuel and Elizabeth set off for a new life in South Africa. This was a time when places like Australia, New Zealand, North and South America and South Africa were attracting many whose families had been firmly rooted in Cornwall for generations.

Details of the voyage to South Africa are not known but it would have been a long and arduous journey. The 1850s was an era when steam-powered vessels were still in their relative infancy and a lot of ships plying the emigrant routes still relied on sail. Whatever the power behind the vessel, it was still a journey of several weeks, with only perhaps a refuelling stop for coal or fresh food and water to relieve the constant swaying motion of the boat.

Soon after their arrival, Emanuel began work at a lighthouse near Newland just outside Cape Town. Lighthouses and other warnings to shipping would have been familiar to him as they had long been a feature around his home on the Cornish coast. The Killigrew family of Arwenack, who we have briefly mentioned above had, as far back as the year 1619, provided a guiding light for shipping at The Lizard and although this was later abandoned for financial reasons, a permanent lighthouse was in operation there from 1751. This and the addition of a lighthouse at St Anthony Head at the entrance to Falmouth harbour in 1835 guided many ships away from the notorious Manacles Rocks and other rocky shores along this part of the Cornish coast. Undoubtedly Emanuel would have seen both of these, particularly St Anthony as its beam of light shone across the bay to his home on the coast at Helford.

The couple's first child, Mary Jane, was born on 24 February 1851 and the family settled into their new life many thousands of miles from Cornwall. The job of keeping the light burning in the lighthouse was a very important one and Emanuel often had to stay at his work for days on end if the weather was stormy as his light could mean the difference between life and death for sailors and their passengers out at sea. This was in the days of often unpredictable lights, long before the days of electricity. During these times, Elizabeth would visit him, taking meals to him while he worked.

Then one day in 1853, about two years after their arrival in South Africa, Elizabeth left Mary Jane in the care of a hired servant woman, known as 'the Gypsy', and attended a meeting conducted by Mormon Elders. This was to prove a turning point in her life.

The Mormon faith was new to South Africa at this time. Mormon president, Brigham Young had called upon 106 men at a special conference in the Salt Lake Valley in August 1852 to leave their wives and families and go on missions to countries around the world. Three of these, Jesse Haven, William Walker and Leonard Smith were sent to South Africa, arriving there in April 1853.

Exactly what attracted Elizabeth to the Mormon Church is not clear, perhaps it was because of the long hours she spent alone whilst Emanuel was working, perhaps it was the novelty of something new to be discovered, but perhaps the tragic events of her early childhood when her father and three siblings had died still haunted her and she hoped the church could offer some support and even some answers. Whatever the reason she, like the other followers and the Elders of the faith, overcame abuse, threats and persecution to pursue their beliefs. Whenever the opportunity permitted, Elizabeth attended meetings and felt compelled to learn all she could about this fascinating new religion. Her attendance at these meetings was at first a secret from Emanuel but soon she was sharing with him the teachings of the Elders. He, however, wanted nothing to do with her new beliefs and this spelt the beginning of a rift in their relationship which would never heal. Their second child, a son, Thomas, was born on 28 December 1854 and the family history records in Salt Lake City show that he was blessed on 3 June 1855 by Elder Thomas Weatherhead, assisted by Elder Nicholas Paul, himself a builder by trade who had been one of the first converts to the faith in South Africa in 1853. The entry confirms Elizabeth as the child's mother and also that the father (Emanuel) was not in church. Elizabeth had been preparing for her own baptism into her new faith for some time under the guidance of Elders Nicholas Paul and Jesse Haven and on 27 May 1855 she entered the water of baptism. Emanuel could still not understand her great feelings of joy and her new beliefs. Records recall that Mary Jane, their eldest child, was blessed on 3 June 1855 at the age of four years and four months – again the entry reads 'father not present'.

A third child, Susan, was born on 14 April 1856 and was blessed as an infant in May of that year. Another daughter, Eliza, who was born prematurely was also blessed as an infant but sadly died at the age of just two months in July 1859. The rift in his family caused by Elizabeth's new faith and now the death of his poor infant daughter had a profound effect on Emanuel. He could not accept the loss of a daughter or the new religion of his wife and he sought to find comfort in drinking heavily.

This inevitably led to even more problems and for over a year, Elizabeth tried in vain to help him and keep her family together but it seems to have been a hopeless undertaking. She sought the advice of Elder Nicholas Paul, by now branch president, and other Elders of the Church. Their counsel was that she should leave Emanuel and journey to the Salt Lake Valley, centre of the Mormon faith in Utah. This was yet another test of her faith. Despite her husband's lack of understanding and sympathy to her new way of life and his recent problems with drink, there must still have been some deep feelings and hope for him, a hope that they might, somehow, begin again and be together as a family. However, it was not to be and so she began secretly to sell her possessions, her handicraft and needlework at which she had excelled since childhood, and eventually saved sufficient money to fund the trip to America. Emanuel soon realised what she had planned and made every effort to change her mind. He was so frantic to save his family and keep them in South Africa that when he found out that the departure date was imminent, he took his only son, Thomas, away several miles to the safe keeping of an elderly native woman. For a whole week Elizabeth made anxious enquiries of Emanuel and all her friends to try and find the child and finally, with the help of her servant woman, 'the Gypsy', she was able to discover his whereabouts and steal him back. All this was just in time for her to travel the 300 miles or so east to

Port Elizabeth and there on 26 March 1860 to set sail aboard the *Alacrity*, a barque bound for Boston in America with her three surviving children, Mary Jane, aged nine, Thomas, aged five and Susan, almost four years old. The ship was the eighth of a total of fourteen ships which left Port Elizabeth or Cape Town with emigrating Mormon Church members between 1853 and 1865. Of these, nine were bound for either New York or Boston with others coming to England. On this voyage there were a total of seventy passengers, including Elder Nicholas Paul, his wife and six children. After two weeks at sea, the ship stopped at St Helena to replenish stores. As they approached the island, the passenger list increased by one with the birth of Lucy Matilda Bodily, the ninth child of Robert and Jane Bodily. Robert was an Englishman, originally from Northamptonshire who, like Emanuel and Elizabeth, had gone to South Africa to work and had there been converted to the Mormon faith. After replenishing of supplies the ship set sail again across a stormy Atlantic Ocean.

Boston was finally reached after seventy-three days at sea and solid ground must have seemed like heaven itself to these weary souls. It was two weeks later that Elizabeth took the next stage of her journey, a train to St Louis, then on to Florence, Nebraska. By this time she had used almost all of her finances and was left with less than the cost of passage to Utah by ox wagon. Her only alternative was to pull a handcart. These handcart journeys have become legendary in the chronicles of Mormon history. A fund had been set up in 1849 to assist Mormon converts with the expense of reaching their new sanctuary in the Salt Lake Valley. The increasing numbers of converts using this fund over the next few years starved it of its assets and by 1855 the Mormon leader, Brigham Young, decided that the cheapest and quickest way of transporting large numbers of the faithful was by the use of handcarts. These two-wheeled carts were about 6-7ft long overall and about half that in width. Personal possessions up to a weight of 17lb per adult and 10lb per child were permitted on each cart and normally five individuals were assigned to each cart. Even though Elizabeth and most of the others travelling in this way would have had little in the way of personal belongings and keepsakes, it was often the case that many items were discarded to keep the weight down to that allowed for each individual. In addition to the handcarts, each journey was accompanied by ox wagons which carried additional provisions and tents. Twenty people were allocated to each tent for the duration of the journey. It was an extremely difficult means of travel, an extreme test of the faith of all of those who undertook the journey. In 1856, the first full year of the handcart journeys, five such convoys, or companies as they were known, set out on the 1,300-mile trek to the Salt Lake Valley. Of these the first three achieved the distance faster and with fewer problems than had been experienced in the past with ox trains. The last two handcart companies that year were both beset by tragedy. The Willie and Martin convoys left too late in the year to avoid the harshness of the winter weather. Each of these two companies set out with over 500 souls, pushing and pulling around 120 handcarts and accompanied by several wagons plus oxen and cattle. Long before their goal was reached, men, women, children and animals were freezing to death in the desperate cold of the Rocky Mountains in November. Despite the assistance of rescue parties sent out from Salt Lake with provisions, the Willie company suffered the loss of sixty-seven of its original 500 souls whilst the Martin company suffered the loss of 145 of the 570 souls who had begun their journey in late July.

Contemporary reports tell of previously strong men worn down by hunger, lack of clothing and proper bedding pulling their carts with their small children and their possessions on board until the day they simply died from the effort involved. Those who died were buried along the route and place names like Sweetwater, Martin's Cove, Rock Creek and Rocky Ridge are etched forever in Mormon history. In the period from 1856 to 1860 almost 3,000 Mormon faithful made the journey in this way in a total of ten handcart companies. Although this figure represents less than 10 per cent of those who made this journey in the twenty years from 1847 when Brigham Young and his followers first arrived in the Salt Lake Valley, their extraordinary efforts and suffering have become an important part of Mormon history, one which is still recognised and remembered to this day.

The company in which Elizabeth Ould travelled in 1860 was the tenth and final handcart company to make this historic journey. It was led by Oscar Orlando Stoddard, a man born in New York in 1821 who, together with his parents, had been converted to the Mormon Faith some years previously. Stoddard and his father had left Utah the previous year, in May 1859, and walked a total distance probably in excess of 5,000 miles over the ensuing months to locations in Michigan and other states before arriving in Iowa City which was a major gathering point for many who wished to make the journey to Utah. From there they moved on to other locations, the size of their following growing all the time until they finally set off on the long journey westward. Once fully assembled, the company consisted of 120 souls with twenty-two handcarts and six wagons which carried additional provisions and tents. Elizabeth Ould, together with her children and others who had travelled with her from South Africa, caught up with the main company on the third day of its journey and Nicholas Paul, who had been such a guiding influence in Elizabeth Ould's life over the past few years, was chosen as chaplain to the English-speaking portion of the company. Oscar Stoddard, the leader of the company, was to marry soon after the safe arrival of his company in Utah. He married Elizabeth Taylor the American-born daughter of an English couple just two weeks after successfully guiding this last handcart company to the Salt Lake Valley. Elizabeth Taylor and her father had been members of this same travelling company and it appears that she grew close to Oscar after he had cured her of illness during the journey.

Volumes have been written about these handcart journeys and as we have seen, some met with tragedy and great loss of life. The Stoddard company, however, had a good journey and made excellent progress across the plains and mountains to Utah. They averaged well over fifteen miles a day and, according to the journal kept by Oscar Stoddard, never camped in the same location twice, making steady progress each and every day. To walk on modern roads and footpaths for seventy-two consecutive days at an average of over fifteen miles a day requires a degree of fitness, but to do it over rough terrain, without proper roads, pushing and pulling a handcart with your worldly possessions in it was rather more than a simple act of faith for these folk. Perhaps the biggest challenge any of these teams met apart from the weather was the crossing of the many rivers along the route. Some were easily forded but some presented major problems. One such was the crossing of the Platte River near Laramie. The procedure for this and other wide or dangerous crossings was to first of all take across some of the wagons and unload them, returning empty to carry the women and children across, together with the contents of the handcarts as it was impossible to haul a loaded handcart across an often wide and fast-flowing river. The empty handcarts were then pulled across by the men of the company and once on the other side, the handcarts were reloaded and the process repeated until all were safely across, a procedure which often took a whole day or even more to complete.

Elizabeth Ould's journey from South Africa to the Salt Lake Valley in Utah was finally completed on 24 September 1860, almost six months to the day after she and her children had set out on the Alacrity.

Once in her new home, Elizabeth had to find work to support herself and her children. She became housekeeper to William Theobald, a widower with seven children. William was born in Freshwater, Isle of Wight in 1813 and had learned the trade of carpenter in his youth. He had spent some time in the navy before returning to England. He was converted to the Mormon faith in 1848, by which time he had married and had a family. He and his family were soon to set out for the new settlement of the Faithful in the Salt Lake Valley in Utah, arriving by ox wagon in 1854. His wife, Martha, died in childbirth in August 1860 and so it was that only a month or so afterwards, Elizabeth Ould came to him as his housekeeper. The couple were married on 24 November that same year and their first child, a daughter they named Charlotte, was stillborn on 14 August 1861. Later in 1861 William and Elizabeth set out for a new home in Duncan's Retreat, some 300 miles south of Salt Lake, where they lived for ten years. Life here was harsh. The constant flooding of the Rio Virgin River washed away their crops and their orchards and threatened to wash away the entire small community and its houses. One by one the settlers moved away and finally, in 1871, the Theobald family abandoned their home and set out for Toquerville. During their ten years at Duncan's Retreat the size of the family had increased. One child had died as an infant but by the time of the move to Toquerville, Elizabeth's family was now fourteen children, seven of her own and seven of William's from his first marriage.

In 1872, William made a trip home to England to see family and friends and during his absence, child number fifteen, Leonora Caroline, was born on 12 August 1872.

William died on 28 February 1895 at the age of eighty-three. Elizabeth lived on at her home in Toquerville for a further seventeen years and died on 17 July 1912. She lies buried in the Toquerville Cemetery. The journey of the young girl from St Keverne had come to its final resting place.

It was a journey which took her from her native Cornwall first of all to South Africa and then the almost unbelievable trek across wild nineteenth-century America with her small children to Utah followed by her further travels with her second husband. It has been suggested that in her later years she felt a sense of guilt for leaving her first husband Emanuel in the way she did. Certainly her eldest son, Emanuel's son Thomas born in South Africa and taken by his mother to America, felt a strong urge in his later life to seek out his father, a quest which was to prove unsuccessful. Subsequently one of his sons also took up the challenge to find Emanuel, but he too failed despite a lifelong search. One source points to the possibility that Emanuel returned to England, settled near Southampton, remarried and named his first son Thomas in memory of the son he had lost. Sad to say though, that research through census and other records has, so far, failed to prove this theory. The search is ongoing.

Much of the detail of the story of Elizabeth Uren comes from the research and writings of Elaine Olds Hagelberg, a granddaughter of Thomas Ould who took up the search for Emanuel and wrote down much of this story back in 1964. Her writings and permission to tell them here have been given to me by Dick Chamberlain of California whose late wife was a great-great-granddaughter of William Theobald. To them, and to Elizabeth, the handcart pioneer, I am greatly indebted.

fourteen

Black Jack James
The Curse of the Kimberley Diamonds

'I warned him not to go down there, but he wouldn't listen. No, he always had to do it his way. So then I had to go down and dig him out.'

Those were words often repeated in his later years by Richard Pascoe James, born in 1888 of true Cornish mining stock. He was referring to an incident in September 1906 when his older brother William had been killed in Marriott's shaft, a particularly dangerous part of Basset Mine where they were both working. William was newly married and his wife Margaret, known to all as Minnie, was expecting their first child when the tragedy struck. She gave birth to a son shortly afterwards and named him Billie in memory of her late husband. She remarried on 20 April 1912 in St Euny Church, Redruth to John Penrose Prout, a twenty-one-year-old close friend of her first husband. John was the son of James Penrose Prout and his wife Edith, formerly Edith Gripe of St Agnes, whose father was a mine accountant. The Prout family, like the James family, had made money and built a reputation in mining. As well as working in the mining industry in Cornwall, James Penrose Prout had managed operations in Bolivia and Chile. He had been privately educated at the Trevarth School, one of several schools set up in Cornwall in the early to mid-nineteenth century for the private education of the sons of wealthy mining families. Margaret James's roots were by contrast much simpler. She was formerly Margaret Parry who had met William James in South Wales where he was visiting on work-related business and where she was working as a barmaid. This 'class difference' did not go down too well with the hierarchy of the James family but was reluctantly accepted as love, they say, conquers all. John Penrose Prout on the other hand was disowned by his family when he married Margaret. He and Margaret also had one son, Basil, but sadly tragedy was to strike again when firstly Margaret died in 1917 and then John also died whilst working in the Oorgaum Kolar gold mine in India. According to family letters he choked on a sandwich whilst watching a tennis match; another in a string of tragic incidents to strike the James family in two short generations.

The family were originally from the St-Just-in-Penwith area where their history has been traced back to 1646. Even further back than this there are records of James or Jamys family names in the Muster Rolls of 1569, when they could arm themselves with one bow, two bills (a hooked blade with a spike on the end) and a bag sling.

Richard Pascoe James was one of six children; William was the eldest, then twins, Edward Thomas and Richard Pascoe, then Jane May, who died young, Elizabeth and John Henry. They were children of William and Jane James. William senior married Jane Pascoe, daughter of miner Richard Pascoe at St Euny Church, Redruth on 16 March 1882 and the census of 1891 shows the family living at their long-term home at Nancothan House, Back Lane, Redruth, with forty-two-year-old William described as, 'unemployed, living on his own means'. He was one of ten children of Robert and Elizabeth James and the 1871 census shows this generation living at the tenement of Botallack, St Just in Penwith and in common with all the near neighbours, the family are engaged in mining.

The nineteenth century was, as we know all too well, a time when Cornwall's mines were closing fast and many thousands were seeking new employment in far-off places. William James was no exception. Along with his friend Francis Oats, he had left Cornwall to work in the emerging mining industry in Michigan and later he went to South Africa where Oats had also gone and where he was already well established in the diamond mining industry.

The story of Francis Oats is itself one which is well worthy of brief mention. He was born in St Sampson near Fowey in 1848, the son of Francis and Maria. The family moved west to St Just in his early childhood years. His father is to be found working as a baker and grocer in St Just by the time of the 1861 census and very soon after this young Francis began working as a miner at the Balleswidden mine. By the time he was twenty-two he was one of the four mine captains at Botallack mine. The 1873 *Kelly's Directory* for St Just parish lists him together with Francis Bennetts, Henry Hocking and Nicholas Hocking as the four mine captains at Botallack. This same directory also tells us that at this time there were fourteen steam-driven engines operating at Botallack variously controlling pumping, stamping and drawing and that amongst its recent distinguished visitors the mine could boast their Royal Highnesses the Prince and Princess of Wales.

Francis Oats married Elizabeth Ann Olds in 1874 and before long he was away on his mining travels with his close friend William James and others, firstly to Michigan and later to South Africa where he made quite a reputation as a mining man, working his way up to be chairman of the Board of De Beers, succeeding legendary explorer turned businessman, Cecil Rhodes, in that capacity. Oats returned to St Just in the early 1900s and with his fortune earned in South Africa he bought Cape Cornwall and built himself a magnificent twenty-one-bedroomed house there in 1909 which he named Porthledden. He returned to South Africa, intending to stay only relatively briefly but died there on 1 September 1918. Porthledden was later run by his son as a hotel but the venture was never profitable and the house was sold in the 1950s to pay family debts. Recently it has been the subject of a major restoration by new owners.

William James also earned himself a reputation and a goodly sum of money in South Africa and also the nickname Kimberley James, after the area where he was working in the diamond mines.

He returned to Cornwall in the late 1880s and purchased Nancothan House in Redruth. As we have seen, he is listed on the census of 1891 as unemployed but the status did not last long and as *The Cornish Post and Mining News* of 14 May 1892 reported, 'Capt. W. James, a member of the Wheal Basset committee and a large shareholder, who two or three years ago returned from the Transvaal, has secured the appointment of manager'.

This 6ft 4in Cornishman, in itself something of a rarity, was soon to take overall control of the combined mining setts of Wheal Basset and South Frances United Mines. But this was a time when Cornwall's mines were all but gone and by the autumn of 1917, Captain William James had had enough. He wrote in his ledger:

I am leaving the management of Basset mines after nearly twenty six years of misery. I am sorry I had anything to do with the concern. After I was here three or four years I saw what was coming and meant to have finished then, twenty one years ago but I was encouraged to go on for most people said if I left the mine would stop. So foolishly I pegged away for another twenty years only to find that what I prophesied came true.

By this time Basset Mines Ltd had accumulated debts of £23,442 and were in dire financial straits. The total workforce had slipped below 300, about half of what it was ten years before. The company limped on briefly without William James but on 21 December 1918 the workers were given notice, the pumping engines stopped for the last time and the mine was left to flood.

William James died shortly afterwards in August 1921. In an obituary in *The West Briton* it is noted that:

John Henry
James -
— Born 1896

Blundell
School

Cadet

The handwritten caption suggests this photograph was taken at Blundell's School where John Henry James received his education but the cap badge is the Royal Artillery, suggesting it was taken after he received his Commission in July 1915. (My grateful thanks to Rick James of Vancouver, Canada, for supplying this photograph and for permitting its reproduction here).

His death left a gap in the ranks of the old fashioned mine managers like his close friend Capt. Frank Oats ... of a somewhat retiring nature, Captain James had a rough manner but a kindly heart ... unfortunately his final years were far from happy: the family fortunes followed closely upon those of a Cornish tin mine industry in its dying days.

The widowed Jane with her unmarried daughter Elizabeth and grandson Billie were now alone at Nancothan House. Billie's half-brother Basil had been taken back to Wales soon after his mother's death where he was raised by her family. As yet another twist in this story, it would seem that relations between the James family here in Cornwall and the Parry family of South Wales were quite strained following Margaret's death, with the Parry family accusing the James family of 'doctoring' her will, leaving young Basil without his mother's inheritance. Basil never returned to Cornwall, but remained in Wales where he carved a successful career in banking.

The words in William Kimberley James's obituary comparing the James family fate to the decline in Cornish mining were quite prophetic for in addition to taking on this lost cause of a mine and seeing it through twenty years of decline, the family suffered yet more bad fortune than that which we have already mentioned.

As well as the untimely death of his eldest son William in the mining accident of 1906, and the other incidents already recalled, one of the twins, Edward, was killed on 28 October 1917 when his ship the SS *Redesmere* was sunk by a German U boat off Portsmouth.

The other twin, Richard, known to all as Captain Dick James, emigrated to Canada in the early 1920s and it is to his grandson, Rick James of Vancouver Island, that I am indebted for information on the family. Rick takes up the story:

Even though granddad was a gruff old codger, his grandkids always looked forward to him sitting down in his easy chair and recalling his memories as a young man growing up in Nancothan House, Redruth, not far from the Basset mines where his family worked. I remember visiting the imposing two storey stone structure surrounded by its luxurious lawn and garden when I was five years old and thought it must have been grand living there, with servants and all, back when granddad was a boy. With a shock of unruly white hair and piercing blue eyes, granddad told his stories in a peculiar English accent. As a youngster growing up on Canada's west coast in the 1950s, it seemed to me that he sounded like the pirate, Long John Silver played by Robert Newton in the Walt Disney movie, Treasure Island. Still, it didn't take long to realise that it hadn't all been that easy for granddad. To begin with, he and his brothers were sent off to work as hard rock miners by their strict father once they turned eleven. I couldn't imagine myself working long hours underground with pick and shovel at such a young age. But what we wanted to hear about more than anything else were stories about his father, Captain William (Kimberley) James who struck it rich in the diamond fields of South Africa.

The one son we have so far not followed was John Henry. He was born on 21 November 1897 and was to add considerably to the family's troubles as he grew older. He developed fraudulent habits, writing bad cheques against the family's presumed wealth and their local reputation. He was well educated, having attended Blundell's School near Tiverton in Devon, one of the leading public schools in England, paid for with his father's money. Like many of his generation he joined the Army during the First World War. He applied for his commission in July 1915 and by December of the same year he was playing his part in the war in France as a 2nd Lieutenant. He was attached to the 122nd Heavy Battery serving with the British Expeditionary Force. After just six weeks, on 1 February 1916, he was rendered unconscious for twelve hours when a German shell exploded in the town square of Ypres. He returned to England to convalesce. He spent some of his convalescence in the Royal Herbert Hospital in Woolwich, London where he complained of severe pains in the back of the head, fatigue and a lack of power of concentration. His medical report on his discharge concludes that he was still very nervous and shaken, that the injuries were severe but not permanent and the diagnosis was simply 'shell shock'. In this day and age when much more is known about the effects of shell shock and the traumatic experiences of war, much more would probably have been done for him but this was a time when the injured, whether physically or mentally, were generally patched up and returned to the front line as soon as possible.

John Henry returned to the family home at Nancothan House for a couple of months' rest and rehabilitation and also spent a short time convalescing in Ireland. There he hopefully had time to recover from the distress of his injuries. He rejoined the Army from sick leave on 26 June 1916 and was placed on the Special Reserve list but his troubles were far from over, indeed they were only just beginning. 14 September 1916 sees a report which pulls no punches whatsoever right from the off.

Its very first couple of sentences speak of him as one whose conduct and lack of ability render him unfit for his position as an officer in His Majesty's Services. His lack of training had already been highlighted before his period of sick leave. The report on his initial officer training course in 1915 concluded that his map-reading skills were poor, and on the subject of field telephony he was considered very poor and that the subject did not suit him. Despite not being able to carry out what would appear to be some of the basic necessities of an officer in the field, namely read a map or make use of a field telephone he was still sent to France to fight, a decision which in itself seems hard to believe but these were days when many barely credible decisions were made. Upon his return from sick leave he was ordered to attend the junior course at the Heavy Artillery School of Instruction to brush up on his general skills. One course he attended was on the subject of field telephone use and in the examination at the end of the course he obtained just twenty marks out of 100. His instructor, Professor Davidge, reports on him as being disgracefully poor and puts this down to the general attitude he took up as regards the work. It is reported that he made no effort whatsoever to follow the subject.

Lieutenant John Henry James pleaded ill health as his defence for his failings and was consequently placed on sick leave and admitted again to the Royal Herbert Hospital for observation. For some obscure reason he was then promptly granted one month's leave of absence from the hospital. Whether the effects of his shell shock were causing him continuing anguish is not known but it is quite likely that he was not fully recovered. It is not suggested that his previous experiences in France excuse him in any way from his current and indeed future conduct outside official circles but they probably did nothing to help. Some of his wayward actions predated his injuries so they can not be held wholly to blame.

Despite his apparent failure to learn much from any of his training sessions and his consequent lack of ability as an officer, it was not this which got him into the severest of his troubles. He had again begun to pass bad cheques. Two cheques, each for the sum of £2, one to the Royal Artillery Mess and one to a woman who kept a small shop near the barracks, were the first to come to light. He was written to by his senior officer on the matter and replied that he would immediately honour the cheques but he failed to carry out this promise. Meanwhile another cheque for the sum of £4 came to light, this time twice presented and twice returned by the bank to the Royal Herbert Hospital. It was some three weeks later that the sum of £8 in bank notes finally arrived from him to honour these debts. He appeared before his colonel to explain his behaviour and he did not help himself by declaring that he was unaware of the seriousness of his actions. The colonel reminded him that this was not the first time such a meeting had taken place. His service record showed that he had been before his commanding officer for similar offences as early as his initial training in 1915 and that on that occasion he had been severely cautioned as to his future conduct. Lieutenant John Henry James even then had the audacity to suggest he had no recollection of this previous incident until it was suggested by the colonel that the officer who had previously interviewed him should be brought to the meeting to remind him. This, it seems, finally persuaded him that he had been caught out again. It was his commanding officer's opinion that Lieutenant James was 'devoid of integrity and ability'. He recommended that the retention of his officer's commission was 'highly undesirable' and that whilst this decision was being officially reached that he should be 'transferred as of no use to Heavy Artillery'. A very damning indictment indeed.

The outcome of this meeting was that preparations were made for Lieutenant John Henry James to appear before a Court Martial for behaving in a manner 'unbecoming of an officer and a gentleman' but despite his obviously very hostile meeting with the colonel and an impending Court Martial for the offences of passing bad cheques, he continued to do so and his mounting debts to local tradesmen were belatedly settled by his father in Redruth.

His Court Martial took place on 2 November 1916 and for some incomprehensible reason, despite finding him totally lacking of principle and extremely poor officer material, found him not guilty. It may be that his father's settlement of his debts counted in his favour. It may be that given the circumstances of the war in France and not wishing to be seen to have a 'bad egg' in their midst that those responsible saw Lieutenant James's offer to resign his commission as a trade off and a course of action less likely to cause a stir. I don't think it is too hard to imagine the steam coming out of his colonel's ears when he got wind of the not guilty verdict!

John Henry James resigned his commission in January 1917 and returned to the war in France as Private James 34152 of the Royal Berkshire Regiment. For a second time he became a casualty of war when he was gassed but he survived to see Armistice declared in November 1918. He left the Army and returned to civilian life but not, it seems, to his family home in Cornwall, at least not on a permanent basis. It also appears that he continued his bad habits after the war as we find the name John Henry James again associated with fraudulent practice in 1921. Whilst employed as a clerk in London, with an address as the local YMCA, he attempted to obtain £12 commission in advance of being engaged by a would be employer. In his defence he said, 'I did not attempt to commit fraud, but I can not help myself, I am a maniac or something of that sort.' Although there is no absolute proof that this is one and the same John Henry James, it is more than coincidence that the name and the misdemeanour fit his character.

Exactly what happened to John Henry or 'Black Jack' James as he has become known by his family is uncertain. As we have seen, his father, William Kimberley James died in 1921 and in his will he left nothing in direct cash terms to John Henry, probably a good indication that he was exasperated at his son's behaviour.

After the events of 1921 there is a gap until December 1931 when a letter was received by his family at Nancothan House from Messrs Harvey & Greenacre, solicitors of No. 60 Bunhill Row, London which certainly relates to him. It was written on behalf of Mr L. Okell of Currie Road, Durban, South Africa and states that a loan of £650 remained outstanding and overdue, advanced by Okell's brother-in-law Mr Joseph Brokenshaw. Black Jack James had persuaded Mr Brokenshaw to loan him this considerable sum of money, saying that he was soon to receive monies from his late father's estate. The letter continues, 'Mr. Okell suggests that you or the Executors of the estate might, as an act of grace, provide all, or at any rate part of the money against Mr James's future inheritance.'

The reply from Nancothan House sums up the family's feelings:

> We have not known my brother's address for these past eight years and have not been in touch with him and it is with the greatest possible sadness to say that we have not wished to hear from him or of him and that he has passed from the family.

A brief and piercing summary of the family feelings towards their errant offspring.

What Black Jack James was doing in South Africa, when he went there and when and if he returned are all unknown. Perhaps he went there hoping to take advantage of his late father's name and reputation to find employment. Perhaps it was a haven far enough away from encircling creditors to feel safe – we may never know.

His dear mother, Jane James who had survived through all this family tragedy and trauma, lived to the age of ninety-two and died at Nancothan House in 1952. Her executors tried in vain to establish the whereabouts of Black Jack James to advise him of her death but nothing was ever heard of him or from him again.

Did he remain in South Africa? Did he return to England, Cornwall even? Did he continue his globetrotting and fraudulent ways elsewhere?

No one knows for certain, but one possible clue lies in July 1939 when *The Times* ran an item on the meeting of creditors of a certain Captain J.H. James of St Andrew's Mansions, Dorset Street, London which concluded, 'No information was available regarding the affairs of the debtor and if he did not attend soon, there would be trouble.' Is this the last reference to Black Jack, or is the name just coincidence?

That case was left in the hands of the Official Receiver in Bankruptcy, and presumably remains there to this day.

The name of John Henry James appears with others on the family headstone in St Euny Churchyard, Redruth but unlike all the others, bears no date for his death.

He remains a mystery . . . unless anyone knows differently?

Rick James concludes:

It is a tragic tale, according to granddad it was all brought on by the Curse of the Diamonds. Retribution for all the Kaffirs who sacrificed their lives for the white man's greedy lust for diamonds in South Africa.

Other local titles published by The History Press

Folklore of Cornwall
TONY DEANE AND TONY SHAW

This volume touches on the wide variety of legends, songs and stories unique to Cornwall and their relationship with the rugged landscape, from standing stones and tales of sea-monsters and mermaids, fairies and giants. The book looks at pagan ceremonies and old traditions, and the very Cornish love of singing, particularly at the inn!

978 0 7524 2929 8

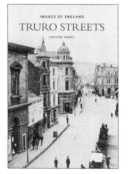

Truro Streets
CHRISTINE PARNELL

In this fascinating new book, illustrated with over 100 old and new images, Chrstine Parnell has researched the origin and development of the city's streets from their beginnings through to modern times. As well as an A–Z gazetteer of Turo's streets, the book combines a more formal history of with many amusing tales, which are sure to delight the reader. Informative and enlightening, Truro Streets will evoke nostalgic memories to the residents and visitors of this beautiful Cornish city.

978 0 7524 4371 3

Haunted Cornwall
PAUL NEWMAN

For anyone who would like to know why Cornwall is called the most haunted place in Britain, this collection of stories of apparitions, manifestations and related supernatural incidents around the Duchy provides the answer. From heart-stopping accounts of poltergeists to first-hand encounters with ghouls and spirits who haunt prehistoric graves, Haunted Cornwall contains a chilling range of ghostly phenomena, including a vanishing house at Bossiney and a phantom stagecoach on the Mevagissey road.

978 0 7524 3668 5

Pirates of the West Country
E.T. FOX

Discover the handful of true West Country pirates of the past and also those that voyaged from the West to the Caribbean and Indian Ocean in this compelling history. Herein lies a true account of piracy, often called the 'oldest trade afloat'. Indeed, it is older than the golden age represented in the literature of Stevenson and Barrie, and more widespread than portrayed by Hollywood. These true tales of pirates operating from places such as Lulworth Cove, Plymouth Hoe and Corfe Castle inspired the pirate fiction we know today.

978 0 7524 4377 5

If you are interested in purchasing other books published by The History Press, or in case you have difficulty finding any History Press books in your local bookshop, you can also place orders directly through our website

www.thehistorypress.co.uk